# Infinity Walk

## Preparing your mind to learn!

## Deborah Sunbeck, PH.D.

**J**

**Jalmar Press**
**Torrance, California**

**Infinity Walk**
Preparing your mind to learn!

Copyright© 1996 by Deborah Sunbeck, Ph.D.

Jalmar Press
Permissions Department
P.O. Box 1185
Torrance, CA. 90505-1185
(310) 816-3085  Fax  (310) 816-3092
E-Mail: blwjalmar@worldnet.att.net

---

**Library of Congress Cataloging-in-Publication Data**

Sunbeck, Deborah.
    Infinity walk : preparing your mind to learn / Deborah Sunbeck.—
2nd ed.
      p.  cm.
Includes bibliographical references and index.
ISBN 1-880396-31-9
    1. Learning, Psychology of.   2. Learning disabilities—Treatment—
United States.   3. Left and right (Psychology)   4. Perceptual-motor
learning.   I. Title.
LB1060.S88 1996
153.1'5—dc20
                                      96-987
                                        CIP

**20+YEARS**
AWARD WINNING
PUBLISHER
**P**

**Published by Jalmar Press**

**Infinity Walk**
Preparing your mind to learn!

Author:                Deborah Sunbeck, Ph.D.
Editor:                 Susan Remkus
Project Director:      Jeanne Iler
Production & Design:  Andy Barnes/Electronic Publishing Services, Inc.
Cover concept:       Jeanne Iler

Manufactured in the United States of America

Second Edition printing: 10 9 8 7 6 5 4 3 2
**ISBN: 1-880396-31-9**

# Infinity Walk

## Preparing your mind to learn!

J

Jalmar Press

# Foreword to Infinity Walk

In an age of multiplying educational needs, limited financial resources, and increasing discord regarding solutions, we are faced with an unprecedented variety of exotic beliefs about educational practices, human development and learning, and essential truth.

As a professional in clinical practice, I bear a responsibility for guiding parents, educators, and other professionals. To effectively guide people toward sensible, wholesome, and fruitful practices, I must sift among and examine the many approaches lauded for results. The expanding array of theories, treatments, and "cures" includes approaches that are novel, exotic, and traditional. Ironically, all the advancements to date have complicated for many people their search for solutions to educational, learning, or behavioral problems.

My evaluation and systematic analysis of educational recommendations and practices incorporate these criteria:

- Congruence with scientifically established knowledge about human development and learning

- Applicability across populations and accommodation of individual differences

- Measurable improvement in the real world

- Learning that generalizes and continues

- Consonance with the learner's visceral and spiritual experience of life

- Enhancement of aliveness and sense of well-being

*Infinity Walk* encapsulates all of these criteria. This book provides extraordinary insight on neuropsychological foundations and common experience. My initial skepticism was quickly dispelled by Dr. Sunbeck's cogent and straightforward presentation of tangible scientific principles. After reading several pages of *Infinity Walk,* I became aware of a familiar feeling I get on those infrequent but precious moments when I encounter a new experience which rings true with all that I know to be real. Spurred by initial excitement, I read further, and was touched by Dr. Sunbeck's ability to reach into my personal and clinical experience. *Infinity Walk* validated so much of my professional work over the past 20 years. Moreover, I just *knew* that Dr. Sunbeck's descriptive models would assist people (including many of my patients) in understanding themselves and overcoming obstacles to learning and fulfillment.

In theoretical terms, Dr. Sunbeck presents a format for understanding how nonverbal and symbolic/representational learning interact. Her *Infinity Walk* techniques provide practical and effective methods for developing the necessary skills to link sensory experiences and "inner" life with the conventional realities of symbolic representation: written language, rules, schedules, logic, organizations, and sequential memory.

For the population of capable individuals who are frustrated by neuropsychological differences of imbalances, *Infinity Walk* is a path to actualizing potential. Parents and teachers of such students know the agonizing refrain, the "he has so much ability, can do so many things well, but it doesn't show in schoolwork." These individuals may be heartened by Dr. Sunbeck's breakthrough formula: Oneness + 2-dimensional representation + 3-dimensional experience = Unlimited Potential.

Two decades of practice in the fields of psychology and education have sensitized me to the developmental gaps which separate 3-dimensional experience from 2-dimensional representation. Psychometric studies, case histories, and clinical observations of many people reveal marked discrepancies between their depth of experience, resourcefulness, competence, and effectiveness in many areas of life and their difficulties in achieving mastery of the "shorthand" our society uses to transmit information — the compression of ideas and events into symbolic form. Many people with learning difficulties are natural and fluid in 3-dimensional qualities: sensory richness, inner resourcefulness, creativity, and ability to look at life from different points of view. Yet they struggle in translating and integrating these perspectives with 2-dimensional aspects of life that are representational: symbolic notation, codes, sequential memory, print-and-language oriented communication, convergent deduction, and focused attention.

Interestingly, there are learning-different people who are much more 2-dimensional than 3-dimensional. As a wise man said about people who live in their heads, "You can't eat the menu." Reaching potential remains very much a matter of balance. *Infinity Walk* helps people develop and maintain balance. Dr. Sunbeck's conceptual framework and sensorimotor training resonates with the methods I use in clinical neuropsychology — specifically, neuropsychological retraining and EEG biofeedback.

Both of these techniques accomplish the stimulation of deficits and the integration of hemispheric functioning so that the whole brain can work in coordination with the rest of the nervous system. Whereas neuropsychological retraining (based on the work of Dr. Ralph Reitan and Dr. Deborah Wolfson) involves specialized teaching targeted to specific cognitive deficits, EEG biofeedback uses a cybernetic learning paradigm to teach the brain to self-regulate its "housekeeping" and higher-order functions. EEG biofeedback teaches people to modulate and control the brainwave frequencies which influence capacities for particular activities and experiences. Dr. Sunbeck has catapulted this science to a new level of common understanding; she has stratified the variations of neurophysiological response into stairsteps for progressive learning and sensorimotor integration.

*Infinity Walk* combines elements from many disciplines. It draws from established theoretical bases and it outlines practical, inexpensive techniques that produce gratifying and lasting results. Within a context of self-regulated learning, *Infinity Walk* allows learners to pace themselves and to integrate the wholeness of their experience while acquiring new abilities.

In an age of finger-pointing at the causes of education problems, Dr. Sunbeck has instead put her finger on a direct path to solutions. I recommend *Infinity Walk* to our clients, and I enthusiastically endorse it among medical, teaching, and help-ing professionals.

*Mark Steinberg, Ph.D.*
*Clinical, Educational, and Neuropsychologist*
*Director of The Learning Studio, San Jose, CA*

# Table of Contents

## MAIL-IN FORM

# Deborah T. Sunbeck, M.A., PH.D.

Deborah T. Sunbeck, M.A., PH.D., is a licensed psychologist in private practice in upstate New York. Her professional training includes clinical hypnosis, psychotherapy, and psychophysiology research. Formerly on the clinical faculty at the University of Rochester, she has co-authored numerous academic publications in areas of psychophysiology, personality, biofeedback and hypnosis, and academically disadvantaged preschoolers. Dr. Sunbeck teaches Infinity Walk and enhanced learning methods at the prestigious Rochester Institute of Technology. RIT's Alternative Learning Department was one of the first university programs in the country to recognize that creative brilliance and learning disabilities (i.e., personal learning style) are often found within the same person. An Infinity Walk lab with trained staff is available to all RIT students wishing to enhance their sensorimotor skills.

Dr. Sunbeck has been recognized for her work in Marquis's *Who's Who in the East* (1993-1994), and internationally in *The World Who's Who of Women* (1994).

As the daughter of a devoutly religious holistic health professional, Deborah's early life was filled with the wonderment of human possibilities. Her inner life was so rewarding as a young child that she hardly noticed she was having problems learning in school. Her insights on the brain's natural learning process from those early years have helped many children and adults find their own special way to mental excellence.

Years of inner discipline and exploration in the martial arts and meditative practices helped clarify Deborah's understanding of what is possible when body, mind, and beliefs are united and in harmony. Foreign travel to work with medically recognized healers has deepened her respect for the body's ability to throw off physical limitations when one's beliefs transcend limited thinking.

It was out of the richness of Deborah's traditional and non-traditional life experiences that the seed for Infinity Walk formed. As a quiet child who lived in the private world of the mystical, she remembers the frustrations of unsuccessfully forcing her mind to meet early academic challenges. As a graduate student, driven by deadlines, and living for the future, she recalls the inner loneliness that accompanies abandoning the mystical in exchange for academic achievement. Her resolution, allowing her to enjoy and benefit from both realms of reality, is at the core of this book. *Infinity Walk* is the accumulation of Deborah's many years of searching for a wholeness that allows her to live from the best of possibilities.

# Michael DeLuca

## *About the Illustrator*

Michael DeLuca is a young artist who experienced learning difficulties throughout his school years, until he worked with Dr. Sunbeck, at age 14. After Michael's mother placed him in a special education program in early grade school, Mrs. DeLuca was told he was not suited for mainstream academia and might eventually need placement in a "special" school. This perplexed his parents, since they saw him as a very creative child who was highly motivated to learn. For Michael, those frustrating years are filled with memories of not being able to access information he thought he had mastered. Often, he experienced his mind as being in a "daze," and unable to break free into clear thinking.

During a series of 7 one-hour sessions with Dr. Sunbeck, Michael's mind did break free. The changes were so dramatic that his mother said she never would have believed it possible if she had not been present for every session. Michael proved that the mind is a dynamic life force; it is only our limited understanding that holds its potential dormant.

Soon after, Michael passed a re-take of the New York State Reading Competency Test, which he had failed a few months earlier. Then, for the first time in his life, he made honor roll the following school term. With a building sense of confidence, he joined the staff of the school's newspaper, and was elected to Student Council that same year. Upon graduating from high school, Michael was awarded a scholarship to Columbus College of Art and Design.

# Acknowledgments

To my mom and dad for never making me wrong for being different,
and my philosopher uncle for all his shared wisdom.

# Foreword

*"Nothing is as important as an idea whose time has come."*

(V. Hugo)

The study of the brain-mind connection and its link to human functioning has a lengthy history. The creator of Infinity Walk, Deborah Sunbeck, has greatly added to our spiraling knowledge base in this area by clearly explaining how individuals can change old neurological habits, master the possibly limitless potential of our miraculous brains, and reap extraordinary cognitive and creative accomplishments in everyday life. The system Dr. Sunbeck has pioneered is based on decades of scientific research and has been tested in her extensive clinical practice and workshop presentations. Persons of varying ages and backgrounds have reported remarkable successes and breakthroughs by applying the principles of her "owner's manual" for the brain and sensorimotor nervous system.

This program is most timely because of accelerating changes in our society which have produced multiple transitions in the economy, family, education, and job requirements. Body-mind preparation is essential so that individuals can intelligently respond to these stressors. As more and more children and adults are faced with family and work-related crises, they are experiencing powerlessness and emotional barriers that inhibit their learning, achieving, relating, and creating. More and more children are having problems with concentration, motivation, and in learning. More and more adults are facing employment changes and will have to develop new attitudes about themselves along with new habits, skills, and abilities.

The Infinity Walk program empowers the three necessary steps of the natural learning process: (1) Self-belief that change is possible and personally attainable, (2) Self-understanding of the neurological foundations that underlie one's abilities and thought processes, (3) A progressive sensorimotor training program that challenges the mind, senses, and muscles to work together in a sequence of increasing neurological complexity.

Deborah Sunbeck's thesis that "extraordinary abilities develop when we have spontaneous and simultaneous access to all brain functions" is supported by Gardner's research on Multiple Intelligences (1983). These seven types of intelligence include:

body/kinesthetic, visual/spatial, verbal/linguistic, musical/rhythmic, interpersonal, intrapersonal, and logical-mathematical. Each of these divergent "Frames of Mind" is located in different functional regions of the brain. The respective and interactive development of these multiple intelligences is largely dependent on the type and variety of opportunities available for differentiated exercise, expression, and extension (McKee, 1990). Infinity Walk progressively enhances the seven intelligences, using the body/kinesthetic intelligence as its core, and cumulatively building the remaining six intelligences into the program in a natural sequence of practice sessions.

Living in the twenty-first century with its persistent and emergent problems and possibilities will surely require greater development of all types of intelligence. The person who can easily access their brain processes will be more equipped to adapt to changes, solve problems, navigate through multiple data bases, and identify workable solutions and humane strategies.

As more individuals have access to Infinity Walk, greater whole brain functioning could make us more mindful of both the extraordinary diversity and unity of all life. Optimal learning, growth, healing, joy, and creativity could become commonplace! Continued use of Infinity Walk can assist individuals from all backgrounds to experience the thrilling journey of *The Little Engine That Could* when he cautiously began with "I think I can. I think I can..." and ended triumphantly with "I thought I could. I thought I could."

Judith Spitler McKee, Ed.D.
Professor of Educational Psychology
and Early Childhood Education
Eastern Michigan University

(Dr. Spitler McKee is author/editor of 12 textbooks in the field of Early Childhood Education, including *Play: Working Partner of Growth,* 1986; and *The Developing Kindergarten: Programs, Children and Teachers*, 1990.)

# What Others Say About this Book!

*"Infinity Walk* appears ideal for overcoming 'self-fulfilling prophecies,' whether self-engendered or otherwise implanted. This learning tool, developed by Dr. Sunbeck, should be recommended, not only for special problem-solving, but also for improving self-assurance."

> *Dr. George Lombart*
> *Senior Vice President (past)*
> *New York State Teachers' Association*

*"Infinity Walk* has opened doors, . . . bridging the newest information in the field of neuro-physiological research to education."

> *Jackie Czamanske*
> *Learning Disabilities Specialist*
> *Rochester Institute of Technology*

"Dr. Sunbeck's work with integrated learning and optimizing human potential is cutting-edge. The theories and methods underlying *Infinity Walk* make sense out of the hodge-podge of literature on whole brain integration. I highly recommend *Infinity Walk* for learning disabilities and super-learning programs alike."

> *David Harris*
> *Founder, Health Optimizing Institute*
> *Del Mar, California*

"An exceptional tool for the whole body worker. *Infinity Walk* offers complete theory and practical workouts for my clients."

> *Sr. Margaret Ann Lawson, R.S.M.; M.S., Ed.*
> *Licensed Massage Therapist*
> *Rochester, New York*

"*Infinity Walk* changed my son's life. After nine years in special education without success, Michael worked with Dr. Sunbeck for seven sessions. The results included honor roll for the first time in his life, regained self-confidence, and recently he won a scholarship to college."

>*Rosemary DeLuca*
>*Parent of "Michael," featured in chapter one*
>*Upstate New York*

"Outstanding book. Essential to a complete understanding of how children with disabilities learn and how to teach them."

>*Kae Dennis*
>*Law Student*
>*Little Rock, Arkansas*

"I find the idea of *Infinity Walk* fascinating. It is the type of application of hemispheric specialization theory that I wish I had thought of myself. I teach a course on the Psychology of Altered States of Consciousness. I plan to use the Infinity Walk as part of the course. I am amazed by how powerful the process of the Infinity Walk is."

>*Dr. Roger Harnish*
>*Associate Professor of Psychology*
>*Rochester Institute of Technology (NY)*

"Insightful! This is a more in-depth study of mind/body coordination than I have been introduced to in the past."

>*Lloyd Peasley*
>*Musician, Educator*
>*Upstate New York*

---

P A R T   1

---

# The Trail Map

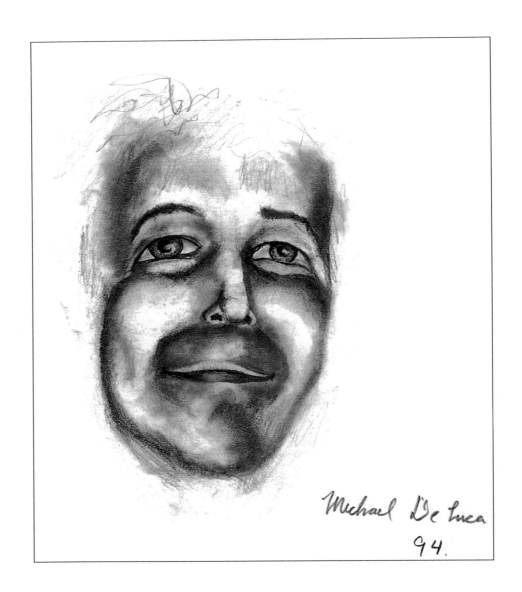

Michael De Luca
94.

# CHAPTER 1

# Michael and the Illusion of Learning Problems

**M**y life had grown comfortable — a successful private practice, active involvement in social causes I cared about, a relaxed home life in a country setting, and lots of adventuresome travel. Then along came Michael. Actually it was Michael's mother, Rosemary, who fits my contact lenses, that started this whole thing. Michael was 14 at the time. He was distraught over some problems at school. His mother, feeling his pain as deeply as if it were her own, couldn't help but talk about him during one of my eye appointments.

Michael had been receiving special education assistance in school since first grade. His mother had been told in those early years that his learning disability was great enough that he may eventually require placement in a special school. Fortunately, that never happened. Michael was embarrassed enough over being different. Nothing seemed to come easy for him — that is, nothing but art.

Michael always had a special talent for drawing. It was his primary source of esteem, and that was the cause of his present crisis. He had just been told that he was not going to be able to take an art studio class the following school year because he had to take an additional reading class, and the scheduling of the two courses conflicted. The reading class was a requirement because he had recently failed the state level Reading Competency Test. The school's hands were tied unless he could pass a re-take of the exam to be given in a few months. This, of course, seemed impossible to Michael.

Michael had always tried his best. He cared about doing well in school and didn't understand why he didn't do well. It was a constant frustration to him. He had learned not to show how much this hurt him, developing an image that outsiders might mistake for underachievement. Losing this art class was just too much for him. He couldn't contain his pain over having his one joy and success in school taken away. Rosemary instinctively knew how serious this loss was in her son's life.

As I sat getting my eyes examined and listened to Rosemary talk about Michael, I began to sense the growing presence of the power of Rosemary's maternal instinct electrifying the room. This woman was speaking from the depths of her being. She was talking life and death, not of the body, but of the spirit of her child. She knew his spirit would die if his art talent was ignored. She knew it would die a little more every time he sat through that extra reading class, continuing to fail at what he couldn't do, feeling punished at losing the one class he loved and could excel in. Rosemary was radiating an incredibly powerful combination of rage over the helplessness of the situation and total love for this boy. I had to offer to help.

Up to this point my private practice had focused on psychophysical concerns — that is, body-mind issues of adults. The field includes such a vast array of challenges that I never dreamed I would branch out farther. A single week might include stress management for an executive just out of bypass surgery; an asthmatic wanting to breathe more freely; a Parkinson patient who wants to keep her joints softer and more flexible through increased self-awareness, imagery, and exercise; a terminal cancer patient desiring to empower his attitude toward the disease and learn pain relief imagery; people with pain and physical limitations that doctors can find no cause for; migraine victims; and so on. I loved my work. People who were referred to me were ready to learn to befriend their strengths and to develop a sensitive relationship with their inner needs. They wanted to learn to be self-empowering, and to break free of limited thought patterns that drained quality from their lives.

I had become so accustomed to the privilege of witnessing seemingly impossible situations turn themselves around that it never occurred to me that Michael's situation might be any different. Fortunately, my graduate training had not included courses in education, so I didn't know the odds against Michael taking charge of his learning disability in such a short time! I just knew that dramatic change was possible when the mind was open to it.

Rosemary and I planned a Saturday meeting with Michael at my home, wanting to avoid any sense on his part of being under a microscope. My first impression as he walked through the door was a lack of physical integration. His walk lacked direction and purpose. His arms hung limp from his shoulder sockets. Only the occasional spark in his eyes betrayed his outer presentation of low energy and casual interest. There was a fire inside waiting to be channeled.

How to get to that fire was the question. What could I say that teachers had not been telling him for the last nine years? I decided to start by telling him about my own childhood memories of school. I told Michael how difficult the early school years had been for me. He started to listen with interest, so I continued. I shared my memories, holding no childhood embarrassment back. Rosemary found her way into the conversation too. She had her own unpleasant memories of her school years. By the end of the first session we were exchanging war stories from school days. We also talked about how our brains "feel." Michael said his felt "fuzzy" most of the time. Rosemary's word for that feeling was "spacey." I had felt "in trance" much of my childhood.

We all seemed to know the feeling of when our brains were really clicking, too. Michael said it felt like diving into a cold swimming pool. We all agreed that when our brains were feeling fully awake, it seemed easiest to learn. Michael had a body memory of what it felt like when things came easily; he just didn't know how to willfully create or sustain it. Our task became clearer as we talked: drilling content would be fruitless with Michael's mind feeling fuzzy most of the time; instead, I needed to concentrate on creating a way for Michael to learn to call forth the feeling his brain had after diving into water. I knew that if he could willfully access this feeling, learning would be much easier for him.

Michael, Rosemary, and I met for 7 one-hour sessions, using the methods you'll find in this book. By the third week he was reporting changes on every level. He received his first grade of 100% correct on a spelling test, his concentration improved, his reading was more comfortable, he felt more athletic in gym class, and even his drawing was becoming more sophisticated. The proof, however, was in his grades. He passed the re-take of the state Reading Competency Test well above the cut-off. The next school term he made honor roll for the first time in his life. He joined the art staff of the school newspaper, and with a renewed confidence in himself, was elected as a representative of school council, all in the same year. Michael's talent flourished, and upon graduating from high school he entered an art college on scholarship.

Michael's personal growth came out of his self-discoveries about his brain: discoveries that empowered him well beyond the scope of new academic abilities. If I had just "fixed" his reading handicap, all we would see today is a spacey young man who can read.

These wonderful changes in Michael were not a new phenomenon to me. I had seen similar stories unfold in my own field of psychophysiology. A very special thing happens when people discover how to overcome what seem to be impossible personal crises. Not only do they gain control over their crises, they gain an awareness of how to be in charge of their own brains. This knowledge can propel them into a rich quality of living previously unknown to them.

Over the years, I have come to the conclusion that many seasoned clinicians arrive at: People don't so much need help going *into* trance, they need to be helped *out of* their own private trances that they have been acting from most of their lives — trances that have prevented them from claiming their full human potential.

The information in *Infinity Walk* can help you open the door to your brain's potential. Rather than allowing your brain to hold you captive in your past, you can learn to take charge of it and create the life you want.

Your very existence is already a miracle. Your brain has infinite potential. I am placing in your hands the owner's manual.

### REFLECTIONS ON CHAPTER 1
### THE ILLUSION OF LEARNING PROBLEMS

1. Think back over your grade school years. What subjects came easily? Which were more difficult? How have your successes and failures in grade school shaped your interests, profession, and self-esteem as an adult? What areas of intellect and creativity have you ignored in yourself since your school years?

2. List things you have wanted to learn or master, but never felt you could, or thought it would be too difficult to bother trying.

3. Is there any reason you have come to believe would prevent you from developing creative and intellectual excellence? If so, where did this belief come from?

4. What limiting beliefs have you been carrying around with you since grade school? List everything you cannot do as an adult because you didn't show potential for it as a child.

5. Michael's most successful days at school were times his brain felt refreshed, like "jumping into a swimming pool." Describe how you feel when your brain is working at its best. Do you believe you have any control over when your brain feels at its best?

# CHAPTER 2

# Extra, Extra, Read All About It! Human Brain Survives Three Lifetimes!

No, no. I'm not talking about reincarnation! I'm talking about your brain. If you are old enough to be reading this book, your brain has already experienced three completely distinct realities since your conception. Each of these realities is so foreign to the others that you could actually consider them to be different lifetimes. Let's take a look at them, because they are the key to understanding your brain and activating its full potential.

When a baby foal is born, it stands up on its feet within minutes, and walks itself over to its mother to check out dinner. That's a pretty sophisticated brain. However, human brains, at birth, are more like newborn baby kangaroos. Except for giving us the ability to cry out, our brains aren't even close to being ready to take care of our needs. This makes us very vulnerable, and leaves us wishing our moms had warm pouches we could crawl into while we learned slowly and comfortably about the world.[1]

---

[1] For an excellent book on nurturing and communicating with your unborn child, read Schwartz, Leni, Ph.D., *The World of the Unborn,* New York: Richard Marek Publ., 1980.

# OUR FIRST REALITY: "ONENESS" IN MOM'S WOMB

Our moms' wombs were our brains' first realities. There, our brains focused on developing our senses of hearing and touch, and concentrated on helping us develop simple muscle movements so we could entertain ourselves by doing acrobatics. This was our entire reality. We knew no other life. But that was okay; it felt great. How wonderful to be comfortably padded with wet warmth, surrounded by softness, without a care in the world. We didn't know there was more to life; and not knowing that we might be missing something left us in a perpetual state of blissful union with all of life as we knew it.[2]

In this first reality, we and our moms were one being. We had no sense of separation or boundary between us and our mothers. We also had no reason to believe that we were not the totality of all existence. We were the "Oneness" that Eastern traditions talk about. Being all of existence left us with nothing to compare ourselves to. This meant that the concept of individuality did not exist, because there has to be at least two people on the planet before we can say we are different from someone else.

---

[2] Pearce, Joseph Chilton. "Mother-Child Bonding," in *Evolution's End: Claiming the Potential of Our Intelligence.* San Francisco: Harper, 1992.

Without the capacity for being different, judgments, labels, test scores, and other forms of categorizing could not exist. So, the concepts of black and white, right and wrong, good and bad, did not exist for us either. This state of "Oneness" and non-judgment felt very safe and blissful, and our brains haven't forgotten that.

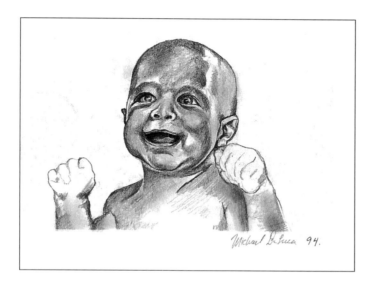

# OUR SECOND REALITY: THE THREE-DIMENSIONAL WORLD OUTSIDE OF MOM'S WOMB

When we emerged into our second reality, the three-dimensional world of our planet, we weren't at all prepared for the shock. The light was painfully bright, and instead of warm inviting moisture caressing us, there was cooler air; not at all friendly. Except for our parents' touch and the familiar sounds of their voices, we felt all alone, as if everything wonderful had been ripped away from us. However, just when we thought all was lost, our brains came to our rescue. They quickly developed our capacities to focus our eyes on our moms and dads, and this brought us comfort.[3]

---

[3] For an overview of how neurologically sophisticated babies are at birth, read Chamberlain, David, Ph.D., "Babies Are Not What We Thought: Call for a New Paradigm," speech given at 10th World Congress of Prenatal and Perinatal Psychology, in Krakow, Poland. Also appeared in the *International Journal of Pre- and Peri-Natal Studies* (4: 1-17); or write Dr. Chamberlain: 909 Hayes Ave., San Diego, CA 92103. Cited in *Brain/Mind and Common Sense,* January 1993.

Our visual development also allowed us to notice other interesting things around us. All of a sudden, we felt inspired to move our bodies over to all those wonderful colors and shapes that were out of our reach! Kicking our arms and legs like we did in our moms' wombs just wasn't getting us across the room, not even when we tried kicking faster and faster. So, once again, our brains came to our rescue, and soon we learned to crawl, and then to walk.

Your brain is an infinite reservoir of potential that lies dormant until you develop a need. You didn't learn to walk just because you were at the correct developmental stage to stand up and walk. Your desire to get across the room, to run into your mom's or dad's embrace, or play with your sister or brother, charged you up with an intense enthusiasm to learn how to walk. Your brain responded to your persistent enthusiasm by creating just the right neuro-chemical pathways you needed to fulfill your desire. This is the way all natural learning occurs.[4]

Let's look a little closer at what our mechanism for learning was back then. What created these intense outbursts of enthusiasm that caused our brains to respond by developing the muscle coordination we needed to: focus our eyes on our parents, walk across the room, hold a spoon, produce words by shaping our tongues and mouths, and be successful at toilet training? The answer is our senses. The three-dimensional world is the realm of pure sensory experience and sensory memory. Sight, hearing, touch, and smell connected us with our immediate environment — not as we were in our mothers, but as separate sensing observers. These sensory connections to our new, very stimulating environment created all kinds of new desires in us.

When you learn naturally, your senses create curiosity and excitement, which act as an electrical catalyst to your brain. This causes your brain to respond by creating whatever mental capacity you need to be successful at your new interest.

However, life isn't all a bed of sensory roses in the second reality. Those wonderful sensory experiences of blissful "Oneness" we had back in the womb were slowly replaced by a growing sense of separateness from our moms.[5] With a little passing of time, and the help of our growing ability to observe through our senses, we began to

---

[4] Kline, Peter. *The Everday Genius: Restoring Children's Natural Joy of Learning.* Arlington, Virginia: Great Ocean Publ., 1988. A good source book on the natural learning process.

[5] Pearce, Joseph Chilton. "Bond Breaking," in *Evolution's End: Claiming the Potential of Our Intelligence.* San Francisco: Harper, 1992.

know ourselves as not only being separate, but being different from everyone else. This made us very vulnerable to judgments from others. We began to sense that being only a few feet tall, with brains as undeveloped as newborn kangaroos, made the world a potentially scary place to be, especially if we were judged as being too different from what adults wanted us to be. All this led to the necessity of our third reality.

# OUR THIRD REALITY: TWO-DIMENSIONAL SYMBOLIC LANGUAGE AND UNNATURALLY ESTABLISHED BELIEFS

Very few people realize we were plummeted into a third, much more restrictive reality while still very young. Few people talk about it. No one prepares us for it. No one acknowledges that it was just as traumatic to us as our original birth into the three-dimensional world. And, no one explains how it has affected everything about our lives since it happened.

I'm putting it here in your owner's manual, so you can understand what happened to yourself when you entered this third reality. Perhaps you will also be able to help children pass through this transition with greater ease than you or I did.

Somewhere in history, humankind decided to band together, to depend on one another for survival and comfort. Hence, the creation of an abstract language, based on strings of visual and auditory symbols, was needed for increasingly more sophisticated

13

interactions with one another. This need probably forced the neurological evolution required for cognitive and language capacities. This abstract, or non–three-dimensional communication system, based on sequencing of alphabet sounds and non-pictorial symbols, became our new means to survival, giving us the skills to be accepted as part of our culture for our protection and personal enrichment. I call this communication system two-dimensional because (1) the written symbols are two-dimensional, having only height and width, and (2) verbal and written language is restricted or diminished by being only an abstraction of the more real and immediate three-D experience.

The survival value of being accepted by a group has become so ingrained in most of us that we start very early in life to accept language as an absolute truth, equivalent to direct three-D experience. We swallow whole the "truths" of our cultures and families, in return for feeling secure in both their implied wisdom and power to protect us.

It was this innate drive to not only survive, but to thrive, prosper, and be loved and accepted by other people that charged our brains with all the electro-chemical energy they needed to propel us into this new reality. Words were at the very root of belonging to this two-dimensional reality, so our young minds had to learn those strange sounds and symbols.[6]

In fact, our desire to communicate with words became so strong that our brains developed special sections in our brain tissue just for language. Just as it had been when we learned to walk, our intense desire to be a part of our new three-dimensional life triggered new brain growth. However, our analogy between walking and talking ends here. The development of the capacity for a symbolic language in the human species required the evolution of our brains beyond the three-dimensional reality that we share with our animal friends in nature.

Our new "higher brain" operated from "man-made" reality, not from the natural laws of life. In fact, everything unnatural to nature operates through this higher brain, which we have labeled the cerebral cortex. What are some of these man-made functions? Some of them are verbal and written language, numbers and other two-dimensional symbols, rules, established beliefs, and time as determined by clocks. Can you think of others?

---

[6] Pearce, Joseph Chilton. "Play," in *Evolution's End*. San Francisco: Harper, 1992. An excellent summary of how the young child's brain prepares itself for language and reading comprehension through visual imagery play.

Words are just man-made symbols for things in our sensory three-dimensional reality. In fact, all symbols must be matched to what they represent in order to be useful, and we do this through a process of defining and labeling. Being able to communicate with each other through symbols certainly has provided us with many advantages over the animal world's more limited sensory communication. So, what's the problem?

Just this. The more primitive part of our brain, in terms of evolution, acted on this new two-dimensional symbolic input the same way it would act on three-dimensional sensory input. It took words as absolute facts, and created automatic habits around all these two-dimensional man-made "truths." Words replaced direct experience and sensory intuition in triggering our brain to develop habitual beliefs and behaviors.

These symbolically derived beliefs that we needed for survival and acceptance were an odd mixture of biological survival rules, like "Don't touch the fire on the stove," and social rules, like "Don't talk when a grown-up is talking." Our brains automatically prioritized all these early language-derived rules for us.

Acceptance into our families and communities was our greatest guarantee of survival at that time, so our magnificent brains responded by deeply embedding rules from important adults into our brain tissues as automatic habits.

So it came to be that all our old childhood survival rules were filed away up there in our heads, under "Rules for Survival." Since we, as young children, couldn't possibly have known that most of those early rules were optional for adults, we didn't know to tell our brains to add subtitles to the file, saying "optional after age ___."

**Your brain's survival instinct cannot distinguish between true danger that is registered by your senses in the three-dimensional world and imagined danger from two-dimensional language input. Your brain's attention to all real or imagined danger always overrides your interest in personal learning and social success.**

We can't blame our brains for prioritizing survival habits for us. They are just being faithful servants to our desires and needs.

Without our brains' capacity to prioritize our survival needs above all else, and to help us develop automatic habits to carry out our needs without having to consult with us constantly, we probably would not be alive today.

Think about it. We'd be in pretty sorry shape if our brains wouldn't take the authority to move our bodies out of the way of a speeding car that we hadn't noticed just because we were talking to a friend. What if we had given our brains the impression that this conversation with our friend had top priority, and we didn't wish to be interrupted be any other sensory input until we were done? We'd be in big trouble.

Our brains always prioritize our automatic habits in what they believe to be our best interests. They never, never, knowingly cause us to do harm to ourselves. Sometimes, particularly in new learning situations, our brains seem to fail us, but this is not really the case. If we look deeply and honestly enough into our "Rules for Survival" file that our brains have been keeping for us, we will always find that our brains were unable to help us with the new experience because they were attending to a real or imagined survival need.

**Once your brain is convinced that a language-generated belief or habit is necessary for successful survival, that belief will always be prioritized by your brain above all new incoming information. This will be true even if the new information conflicts with the original survival belief and is intended to replace the original input.**

As adults, this phenomenon has made for some very illogical thinking and inconsistent beliefs and behaviors in us. It also leaves us with a strange discomforting feeling that we aren't in charge of our own minds. Yet, deep inside, we can also quietly feel our tremendously powerful untapped potential. Somewhere, we sense a vague, intangible memory of our beginnings, when our desires and our brains acted as one in perfect union.

You may be familiar with this inconsistency in yourself. Sometimes you are aware of how clever or creative you really are. Other times you are dismayed with how little confidence or faith you have in yourself. These times are clues to when you and your brain are in agreement, versus when your brain is running on automatic, playing out those old, outdated survival habits you haven't needed in years.

*LET'S QUICKLY REVIEW:*

We all started existence on this planet in a reality of infinite "Oneness," otherwise known as our lifetime in our mothers' wombs. Then suddenly we were propelled through a tunnel into the light, and we were born, or reborn in a sense, into our second reality. This three-dimensional reality is our relationship to life through our senses. The three dimensions, of course, are the height, length, and depth that create the density of all physical matter and objects. Everything in three-dimensional reality can be touched or seen, even if only on a microscopic level. All sensing operates this way. Our ears are touched by vibrations, our eyes are touched by light, and our noses are touched by "scent" molecules floating through the air.

Sometime during our second reality of three dimensions our reverence for our mothers also began to fade. Our mothers were no longer sharing with us in one perfection. Instead they had become solid objects different from our own separate solidness. This was a traumatic experience; but even so, our brains did an outstanding job of helping us acclimate to this second reality.

Our need to communicate with others through language led us into the third reality, that of two-dimensional symbols and pre-determined beliefs. Spoken words took on a reality of their own. They became our beliefs and truths, replacing our immediate perceptual experience and sensory intuitions about three-dimensional life.

But it doesn't end here. The introduction of two-dimensional written symbols into our life was the final blow to our weakened hold on our early three-dimensional sensory life. The impact of written language on our brain has been so powerful in shaping how we think and learn that the topic deserves its own chapter.

### REFLECTIONS ON CHAPTER TWO
### HUMAN BRAIN SURVIVES THREE LIFETIMES

1.  What do you know about your first "lifetime of Oneness" in your mother's womb? Find out what you can about what was going on in your parents' lives while your mother was pregnant with you. Find our everything you can about her labor and delivery of you into the three-dimensional world. Ask for details about your first months of life outside the womb.

    Your brain remembers all this on a cellular level, but can't tell you directly with words, because the language part of your brain wasn't yet developed. Your brain can only represent this very early experience as vague feelings and urges that can leave you confused and longing for something you can't describe. The more you can find out about your beginnings, the more these primitive, pre-verbal feelings will make sense to you. The more they make sense to you, the more you will become in charge of them, instead of them in charge of you.

2. Close your eyes, and imagine what life would have been like if "Oneness" had been your only reality. Remember, your ability to judge, make comparisons, and desire other sensory pleasures, or even to know anything else exists, would not be developed. Take a few moments to quietly feel what it would be like to only know "Oneness." Your brain still remembers, so it will help you feel this "Oneness" memory, if you *let it*. Afterwards, write down how you felt while visiting your Oneness reality.

3. What do you remember about your early sensory reality of the 3-D world? Go through the list of all your senses, and remember as many first sensory memories as you can. For instance, re-experience the first time you tasted lemon; the first flower you smelled; the first starry night, sunrise, and sunset your eyes remember seeing; and the first time you saw, touched, or smelled different animals. Remember all the sounds of nature you may have enjoyed as a child. What sounds can you remember from your childhood home: a clock ticking, water dripping from a faucet, Dad's electric razor, splashing water in the bathtub, children playing in the neighborhood, a neighborhood dog barking? You'll be able to remember lots of sensory memories if you let your brain help. List your favorite sensory memories for taste, smell, sight, hearing, and touch. How many of these still bring back pleasant feelings?

4. Imagine what your life would be like if sensory reality had been your only experience of life. Imagine bathing your senses in all kinds of wonderful experiences without the possibility of labeling, judging, or comparing anything. Imagined your wide-eyed, beaming-smiled pleasure in soaking in one new sensory experience after another, for your entire lifetime. Your brain still remembers, so let it help with this sensory imaging. Afterwards write down what you felt for future reference.

5. Imagine what you would be like if you had continued to develop all your senses through constant awareness, stimulation, and exploration. Imagine how you would experience life if all your senses had been fine tuned and perfected, but you had never lived in a culture that used spoken or written language. Journal your thoughts on this.

6. What rules, beliefs, and facts were you told as a child, through the use of language, that haven't proven to be true as an adult?

7. Read the following list of words: OCEAN, BIRD, ROSE, LEMON
   Now, go back and experience each one slowly through all your senses. For instance, for the word "ocean," in your mind walk onto a beach and feel the warm (or cool) sand between your toes, and pushing up against the arches of

your feet. Feel the salty ocean breeze sweep across your face. Hear the crashing waves and feel the salt water spray over your skin as you approach the water's edge. Hear the sea gulls as they glide above you. Now step into the cool wet sand and feel the ripples left in the sand from the beating waves. Wait for the white foamy water to rush over your feet, as you stretch your vision out to infinity. This is the experience of "ocean." Close your eyes and live it through all your senses. Your brain has the capacity to make it as real as if you were really there, if you let it.

Now do this for the other three words: BIRD, ROSE, LEMON. Notice how these 2-D symbols didn't really come alive until you took the time to experience them through your 3-D sensory memory. The more senses you involved in your memory, the more real you were able to make your experience.

8. Read the following list of words: HOUSE, GARDEN, OAK, POND, RED, DUCK, FORK, SKY, PUDDLE, CAR, SMALL, DIRTY, BRIGHT, SWEET, SMOOTH, SOFT, DARK, OLD, ROBIN, RIPPLE

Now, without looking back, close your eyes and repeat all the words you can remember. Record the words you remembered. Next to each word, write whether there was a special way for you to help remember the word.

Next, go back and create one sensory fantasy from all the words. Use all your senses to experience your "story," just like you did for the word "ocean" in Reflection #7. Take your time and enjoy your sensory creation. When you're done, list all the words you can remember. You should be able to remember many more this time. Later today, recreate your fantasy in your mind, and recall the list of words again. You'll find that long-term memory works better when you store 2-D information as sensory memories than when you are just trying to memorize language-generated information by rote (without 3-D understanding).

# CHAPTER 3

# Written Language:
# The Further Reduction of Our
# Sensory Intuition and the Start
# of Many Learning Disabilities

During a short window in history, humanity experienced an overlap between photographic technology and the existence of simpler cultures unaware of such technologies. Social scientists visiting these cultures reported the natives experienced distress when shown photographs of themselves. The natives believed the photographs had captured their souls, and had to be destroyed to have their souls returned to them.

Imagine if these people could see only three-dimensionally. The photographic paper would appear to have captured, paralyzed, and miniaturized their three-dimensional bodies.

I can still remember my own early childhood, when my eyes would automatically move right into a photograph. Totally ignoring the boundary of the paper, I would enter the picture and see everything in its three-dimensional form. In fact, this is normal for very young children.

You may have had the experience of reading to a young child out of a picture book and having that child continually try to turn the page over before you had finished reading the first side. This was not impatience. This child was searching for the third dimension of the picture, on the back of the page.

*I once read a story book about farm animals to a little boy named Tommy. The picture on the page showed a barn with ducks, and sheep, and a goat outside, in front of an open barn door. Then the story went on to say that the farmer kept the cows and horses inside the barn. However, the opening was painted black to depict darkness inside, so no cows or horses could be seen. Well, this little boy, who had been half asleep, suddenly grabbed hold of this two-dimensional barn. Practically ripping the page out, he turned it over to view the other side. I watched his expression turn from interest to great disappointment and confusion. He looked up at me and asked, "Where are the cows and horses? I want to see inside the barn." Tommy was just beginning his struggle through the transition from three-dimensional to two-dimensional reality.*

## WRITTEN LANGUAGE

Think about what written language would look like if your brain recognized only the three-dimensional world. All the letters and numbers you would be learning would be seen as objects in space, rather than ink on paper. How each of them looked would depend on what side of the object you were viewing it from. In three-dimensional reality, a "d" would look like a "b" if you were standing behind it, or if it had its back to you. A "2" could also look like a "5" doing a handstand. An "n" would look like a "u" diving into a swimming pool. This is how the young mind perceives when first introduced to written language. The errors that children make when learning to print and read all make sense if viewed from different angles in three-dimensional space. In the adult world, the ability to see an object from any angle is considered to be an artist's perspective.[1]

---

[1] West, Thomas G. *In the Mind's Eye.* Buffalo, New York: Prometheus, 1991. Excellent coverage of gifted people with dyslexia, suggesting that their great accomplishments did not come from compensation for their "handicaps," but because they could not, or did not, compensate for their dyslexia, leaving their three-dimensional mind intact.

***Three-Dimensional Visual Learner***

# ABC'S AND 1, 2, 3'S:  A 3-D PUZZLE

I once had the pleasure of working with Jimmy, an eight-year-old boy who was still having trouble identifying simple words with any consistency. Jimmy had already, in his short academic career, changed schools a few times. Each time his parents had hoped it would be a fresh start for him.

The schools' efforts, to this point in time, had been fruitless. This charming young man was failing so badly that he became the joke of each new classroom. His parents couldn't believe he lacked intelligence. At home, he was a verbal, creative, inquisitive child; he kept them on their toes with his challenging questions and insightful comments. To make matters worse, his pediatrician was unwilling to authorize insurance coverage for outside help, because he was sure nothing was wrong with the child. As for the boy, when I asked him at our first session if he knew why he was visiting me, he looked deeply into my eyes, took a slow deep breath, and answered, "Yes. It's because I'm a failure." What a heartbreak! Eight years old, and he already felt like a failure.

To understand what Jimmy and many young children see when first learning to read, try the following exercises. Using the lines as a guide, stand a mirror up so the glass faces the column and row of letters. Position the mirror so the letters are easily seen in the mirror.

The reversed column of letters shows how they would look if you were standing behind them, in three-dimensional space, looking at their backs. The reversed row of letters and numbers shows how they would look upside down.

| | |
|---|---|
| o | |
| l | These letters, when reversed, |
| w | look the same, so they are |
| t | always right |
| x | |
| v | |
| | |
| e | Letters like these are always |
| g | considered wrong when reversed |
| k | |
| | |
| b | These two letters turn into |
| d | each other when reversed |
| | |
| p | |
| q | So do these |
| | |
| N | It's all how you look at it. |
| | Tilt your head left, and the N |
| Z | becomes a Z. Tilt your head right, |
| | and the Z becomes an N. |

2 5 S 5 S 2 5 2 2 S 5 S 2 5 S 5 2 5 5 2 5 S

How fast can you read this line from the mirror, without any errors?

Here are more letters and numbers that can be confused. Can you think of others?

M W   m w   J L   I l 1   E 3   6 9   O 0   7 L   g q

Using a mirror to view letters and numbers can help an adult to understand what a child might see when first learning to use symbols. However, this established use of the "mirror image" explanation of children's tendency to reverse letters (also known as dyslexia), is a two-dimensional understanding.

One of the "second reality" memories I have from early childhood is floating around objects inside my mind, as if I were an astronaut in space. Think about this. If your mind has always lived in the anti-gravity reality of your mother's womb, how could there be up or down, left or right, or any sense of direction at all? Try this. Place the letter "b" in space. As you float around it, the letter changes from "b" to "q" to "d" to "p" to a number 9. You'll also see it from other angles that make the symbol look foreign to you. Such a dynamic view of life is exciting for a child.

Children who manage to save this natural ability to see the world from many angles often make excellent artists, architects, and design engineers. Children who retain the ability to listen in this same way grow up with the qualities needed to be musical composers, insightful counselors, and unbiased arbitrators. However, the early years in school can be a nightmare for these creative children until they find a way to integrate two-dimensional symbols into their three-dimensional perspectives on life.

I know a very successful entrepreneur who writes the number 5 as an upside down 2. That is, as one flowing line, starting at the bottom left, he draws a perfect upside down two. If I hadn't watched David while he was writing, I would have missed it, because the end result looks just like a five. When I pointed it out, he remarked that he had always drawn his five like that. This man, who failed second grade, had been an efficiency expert for a major industry before he unleashed his full creativity into entrepreneuring enterprises.

The explanation for his unusual five is actually quite simple. David had learned the number two first, and immediately noticed that the number five was just another variation of the number two. Being both creative and efficient, he found it more practical to continue to draw two's than learn a new shape.

Unfortunately, by drawing 2's and 5's as variations of the same shape, his young brain confused their meaning when doing simple arithmetic problems.

If his teacher had understood how David's cleverness was causing the confusion, she might have been better able to help him perceive the two numbers as having totally different meanings in the three-dimensional world. Instead, the slip in his logic went unnoticed. Seeing only that he could not correctly add or subtract, the teacher held David back a year. He told me he was emotionally devastated by this embarrassment for years, until he finally discovered the flaw in his logic and corrected the problem for himself.

I have my own memories of attempting to read in the early years. Words just wouldn't look the same from one minute to the next. The letters just wouldn't hold still on the page. Letters like F or K were easy to recognize, no matter what direction I viewed them from. This would be no different than your ability to recognize a friend from the back or front, even though the two views look different.

Probably the worst letters were the ones that looked like each other from different directions. Without having one consistent viewpoint to see all letters from, I would never know if I was looking at a "b" or a "d"; I just knew the letter was one or the other.

Some of the letters in the English alphabet actually made it more difficult for me to establish one consistent point from which to view all the letters. These are the letters that look the same from front or back, letters like "i," "o," "l," "x." These letters made it valid to continue reading from behind them.

Ten of the 26 alphabet letters, when seen in capitals, look the same viewed from the back as they do when viewed two-dimensionally from the front. They include four vowels. Eight of the 26 alphabet letters, when seen in the lower case, share this same confusion. They include three vowels.

A  H  I  M  O  T  V  W  X          i  l  m  t  v  w  x

How is a child to know that written language is supposed to be a two-dimensional task? How is our very capable brain supposed to design a new visual ability for us to recognize two dimensions consistently, without this information?

The letters "i" and "l" presented an additional problem for my eyes. More than any other letters, they gave me no clues as to where I was standing when viewing them; my viewpoint could have been anywhere in the 360 degree circle around them, and they would still look exactly the same. At least with letters like "t" or "o" I knew I had to be either in front or in back of them. These vertical straight lines would completely throw off my sense of direction in scanning a word. My eyes would lock on to an "i" or "l" and start spinning around it, not sure when to get off, and which direction to head in from there! Needless to say, by the time I unlocked my gaze from one of these vertical poles, I had lost the word and the meaning of the sentence.

I don't know why some of us have more trouble adjusting to two-dimensional visual perception than others. (No one does.) There is some evidence to suggest a genetic tendency toward learning disabilities, so it would be easy to suggest that difficulty in viewing two dimensions is genetic.[2] However, I have found that most learning disabilities that involve written language disappear as soon as the person discovers the relationship between two and three dimensions, and develops a mastery over the two-dimensional symbols of letters and numbers. So, if it is a genetic tendency, it may also be an easy one to overcome, or compensate for.

# TWO SOLUTIONS

Let's look at two possible solutions, both feasible.

## *Solution # 1*

The first is to actually "fix" the letters and numbers that are causing the problem in the first place. There is some evidence to suggest the possibility that dyslexia is specific to the Western culture alphabet. For instance, reading disabilities are rare among young Japanese students. "In Japan, children are usually taught two different scripts — first, the *Kana,* in which the symbols correspond more or less to syllables and are combined to form words, and later the *Kanji* script, in which the symbols are based on Chinese ideographs and stand for whole words. In neither case is there any confusion created by reversing a symbol since no two symbols are mirror images of each other. There can be no mirror-image confusion in reading the symbols."[3]

---

[2] For thorough reviews of the genetic and organic perspectives on learning disabilities read: Galaburda, Albert M., M.D. (Ed.), *Dyslexia and Development: Neurobiological Aspects of Extra-Ordinary Brains,* Cambridge: Harvard University Press, 1993; and Galaburda, A.M., "Neuroanatomic Basis of Developmental Dsylexia," *Behavioral Neurology* 11:1, 1993; and Galaburda A.M. (Ed.), *From Reading to Neurons,* Cambridge, M.I.T. Press/Bradford Books, 1989; and Lubar, J.F., Bianchini, B.A., et al., "Spectral Analysis of EEG Differences Between Children With and Without Learning Disabilities," *Journal of Learning Disabilities* 18:7, 1985.

[3] Corballis, M. and Beale, Ivan. *The Psychology of Left and Right.* Hillsdale, New Jersey: Lawrence Erlbaum Publ., 1976. Cited research study: Mikita, K. "The rarity of reading disability in Japanese children," *American Journal of Orthopsychologia,* 1968, 38, 599-614.

In addition, disadvantaged inner-city children who had been unable to learn reading and writing without significant dyslexic confusion were able to master both when taught to read and write using Chinese characters. The characters were written left-to-right in the English manner, eliminating the possibility that a change in the direction of scanning solved the dyslexic confusion.[4] (Chinese characters are drawn vertically.) Again, the root of the problem appears to be in the English symbols themselves, and certain printing types can make the dyslexic confusion even worse.

Publishing companies use a variety of printing types when typesetting text. Why not use a printing type in children's books that would avoid creating this early dyslexic confusion between three- and two-dimensional vision. We build wheelchair ramps for the physically handicapped to remove barriers that would otherwise prevent them access to broader life experiences. A printing type that could be accurately recognized by the young three-dimensional visual learner would remove the written language barrier for potentially dyslexic children. What would such a printing type do for children who have no tendency toward reversing letters and numbers? Probably only a lot of good. It could mean that children would never need to give up their three-dimensional visual perspective on life to excel during their early academic years.

The illustration below shows how a dyslexic-free alphabet might look. Notice that every symbol can be understood now, without being penalized for viewing them three-dimensionally. Every letter can be correctly identified from any angle in space.[5]

***Dyslexic-Free Alphabet***

---

[4] Ibid. p. 163.

[5] Permission must be obtained from the author and Jalmar Press before using this alphabet for any commercial or profitable venture.

This three-dimensional alphabet is built on simple rules to help the new reader problem-solve the correct position of each letter in print, rather than having to learn each shape by rote. (The following chapters explain the importance of not forcing rote memory too early onto the young creative mind.) All rules are based on curves and lines. Curves always start with movement to the left; lines always start with movement right or down. The traditional English alphabet has no such logic to its structure, so the child's brain is forced to address rote two-dimensional visual memory before it is ready.

Curves - Left         Lines - Right or Down

## *Curves*

Rule 1.      All letters that start with a circle or a curve are drawn to the left (counterclockwise).

C S d e f

Rule 2.      All curves that finish off a letter are drawn to the left.

J S g j

Rule 3.      When a letter is constructed around a vertical line, circles are always placed to the left of the line.

a d g q

## *Lines*

Rule 1.      Short lines are always drawn toward the right.

E P Z q

Rule 2.      When a letter is constructed around a vertical line, shorter lines and angles are always to the right of the vertical line.

K R h n

If you are currently working with dyslexic children, determine which symbols they reverse or confuse by observing their writing, and listening to their reading and spelling. Remember, their errors do not need to be consistent. The three-dimensional mind is viewing the letters from multiple perspectives, so these children will have a certain percentage of "accurate" viewpoints. I put "accurate" in quotes here because the three-dimensional mind doesn't judge one visual angle as better than another. It is the desire to receive the benefits derived through social conformity that motivates these children to see the alphabet only as others do.

## Solution # 2

The second solution would be to educate our children on the problems with the English alphabet, and point out the differences between two-dimensional viewing and the "artist's" perspective of life. This way children would be encouraged to maintain their more creative three-dimensional perspective on life while being cautious not to confuse that perspective with two-dimensional written symbols.[6]

We would still have to take into account that some children's brains are not ready to see two-dimensionally before eight and even ten years old. This is especially true for males,[7] which is why the majority of students labeled learning disabled are boys. The reason for this early developmental difference between young males and females is highly complex, but can be understood in the context of human evolution, and the separate roles males and females needed to take during more primitive times in history. We can begin to understand this difference in language maturation in the brain between young girls and boys by realizing that there is up to an 86% overlap in the brain for language and motor sequencing. There was a time in history where survival of a community meant that males used this brain site to master hunting skills requiring refined motor sequencing abilities, while females used the same brain tissue to communicate and network daily on the sharing of work and the smooth running of the community.[8]

---

[6] There are many good programs and books today on helping children learn through imagery. Some of them include Goode, Caron B. and Watson, Joy, *The Mind Fitness Program for Esteem and Excellence,* Tucson Arizona: Zephyr Press, 1992; Galyean, Beverly, *Mind Sight: Learning Through Imaging,* Berkley CA: Center for Integrative Learning, 1988; Bagley, Michael T., *200 Ways of Using Imagery in the Classroom: A Guide for Developing the Imagination and Creativity,* New York: Trillium Press, 1987; Vitale, Barbara Meister, *Unicorns are Real: A Right-Brained Approach to Learning,* Torrance, CA: Jalmar Press, 1982; Rose, Laura, *Picture This: Teaching Reading Through Visualization,* Tucson, Arizona: Zephar Press, 1991; Stoddard, Lynn, *Redesigning Education: A Guide for Developing Human Greatness,* Tucson, Arizona: Zephyr Press, 1992.

For educators and parents who might think that slowing down the pace of teaching written language to young sensory minds would disadvantage these children, a lesson here can be learned from the Cherokee Indians.

The Cherokees of the Great Smokey Mountains[9] were a peaceful nation. More advanced than some of the other Indian tribes, they had already developed a sophisticated society before Europeans began to settle in the United States. Early settlers found the Cherokees building permanent houses, weaving cloth, making clay vessels, and having an organized and effective political confederation. The Cherokees helped the early English and Scottish settlers learn to harvest the rich resources of the land. In exchange these settlers taught the Cherokees about their own powerful God as represented in their Bibles.

The Cherokees called these books the "talking leaves," and believed them to be a special gift from God that only the white people had been privileged to receive. One Cherokee man, named Sequoyah, thought differently, and he set about creating a written alphabet for the Cherokee language. Having no knowledge of the rules of written language, he made many attempts over a number of years until he settled on a simple alphabet that represented each sound as a different mark on the paper.

During the years that Sequoyah worked on creating the Cherokee alphabet, he and his family were ostracized by the Cherokee community. His people believed he was going to bring evil down on them by upsetting God. Even his wife, on one occasion, burned the accumulation of all his written efforts, in her frustration and fear.

Once the alphabet was complete, the Cherokees had a change of mind, and all wanted to learn to read the "talking leaves." Sequoyah traveled to the different Cherokee tribes teaching the adults how to read and write the symbols. Here's the amazing part. It

---

[7] Ornstein, Robert, and Thompson, Richard F. *The Amazing Brain.* Boston: Houghton Mifflin, 1984; and Benson, D. Frank, and Zaidel, Eran. *The Dual Brain.* New York: The Guilford Press, 1985; and Springer, Sally P., and Deutsch, Georg. *Left Brain Right Brain.* San Francisco: W.H. Freeman & Company, 1981; Calvin, William H. *The Throwing Madonna: Essays on the Brain.* New York: McGraw-Hill, 1983.

In contrast, Levinson, Harold N., M.D., in *Smart But Feeling Dumb,* New York: Warner Books, 1984, believes that the incidence of male dyslexics equals that of female dyslexics, but males are referred more for treatment because of acting out their frustrations more than females.

[8] Calvin, William H. "Did Throwing Stones Lead to Bigger Brains?" *The Throwing Madonna: Essays on the Brain.* New York: McGraw-Hill, 1983, pp. 28-42.

[9] Underwood, Thomas B. *The Story of the Cherokee People.* Cherokee N.C.: Cherokee Publ. 1961. (P.O. Box 256, Cherokee, N.C., 28719)

is recorded in Cherokee history that the new written language was learned in a minimum of three to four days by the brighter of each tribe! Soon, the Cherokees had their own printing press, and were translating English newspapers, books, and U.S. government policies for all their people to read. Learning a phonetically based written language turned out to be a simple process for the developed adult mind of a people who are known to have rich sensory abilities. (The Sequoyah Redwoods were named in honor of the greatness this man brought to his people.)

Let's not worry so much about whose child is reading and writing earliest. Let's not shame our children for not keeping up with other children's reading development. Let them have their rich sensory experiences, and the rest will follow naturally, in due time. Force them too soon, and their efforts to master 2-dimensional understanding may never take root.

*REFLECTIONS ON CHAPTER 3*
*WRITTEN LANGUAGE*

1. What are your own memories of learning written language?

2. If you could be Emperor or Empress of Education for the Day, and make any change in the way children are educated in the schools, what would you change?

3. Think back over your own school years. How would you have liked to be taught the different subjects that you remember? Who was your best teacher? What made this teacher so good? Who was the worst? Why?

# Oneness + 2-D + 3-D =
# Our Unlimited Potential

Optimal learning occurs when we are most in charge of our brains. Extraordinary abilities develop when we have spontaneous and simultaneous access to all brain functions.

There are many different ways to be intelligent or gifted, without having to develop our full brain potential. Many people find one way to express their mental or creative abilities, and then they stop learning. They become very good at one or two things, and then develop their personal or professional identity from their success in these particular limited aspects of life.

On the surface, they may show confidence and satisfaction with the life they have created. However, as most clinicians know, the phenomenon of mid-life crisis reveals the truth. Many of these people's narrow lives did not come to them through a conscious free choosing. They willingly admit giving thirty years to an expertise that didn't even excite them, just because it was something they were good at when they were young. Others come to realize that those years of narrow focus were meant as a distraction from getting to know themselves and others, accomplished by abandoning their sensory connection to three-dimensional life.

When people narrow their focus of learning too much, they lose their opportunity to develop their brains' capacities for brilliance and creative excellence. This includes lost potential in their own area of concentrated focus.

## EMPTY WIT

I counseled a young teenager, 15 years old, for just this problem. Dan was under the impression that he was very bright because of being verbally precocious since pre-school. His mother asked him to see me, because his grades in math seemed to be getting worse over time. Dan, himself, had reached a point of being concerned that his poor math grades would keep him out of the better colleges. He had high aspirations for himself, and had a number of career desires, all involving excellent verbal skills.

As Dan sat talking with me, it became obvious that he judged intelligence by verbal abilities, rather than realizing that it was only one kind of mental ability.[1] He thought subjects like math were boring and unnecessary. Dan was sure it was a waste of his time to learn math formulas and solve math problems that he would never use again. He was under the misconception that his future career would be totally unrelated to math abilities. He was very wrong. Let's see if you can guess why, from how I describe Dan to you.

Dan talked pretty much non-stop through our session, spending a great deal of time trying to convince me he was right about math being useless to him. He would often ask me a question just to continue talking right over my answer, as if the question was to stimulate his own thinking rather than to gain someone else's input. He tried to use humor and verbal wit to win me over. When that didn't work he attempted to strengthen his position with cleverly phrased sarcasm.

A number of times I had to refocus him back to the purpose of his visit: He wanted to do better in math so he would be accepted by an excellent college. For a moment then, he'd show some awareness that his arguments were irrelevant and unhelpful to his goals. However, within minutes he would lose his fleeting logic, and go back to trying to impress me with his debating skills.

---

[1] Gardner, Howard. *Multiple Intelligences: The Theory in Practice.* New York: Basic Books/Harper Collins, 1993. Dr. Gardner has identified seven types of intelligences: verbal/linguistic, visual/spatial, body/kinesthetic, logical/mathematical, interpersonal, intrapersonal, and musical/rhythmic.

To not leave you hanging, he did finally respond to my firmer and firmer confrontation, and made the choice to let his father tutor him in math; a choice he had not been utilizing.

Can you guess how Dan was restricting his intelligence by resisting academic subjects that did not interest him? He was not letting the qualities of his brain related to common sense problem-solving and disciplined attention span develop in himself. Without these abilities — both related to math problem-solving — he was left with an infinite string of clever words that were useless to his present goal. If he had allowed this to keep him out of a good college, he may have missed his chance to fulfill his career dreams.

Like Dan, most of us have disabled our capacity to learn one or more specific skills by our attitudes toward those skills: we have created a learning disability. Surprising? This shouldn't be. A learning disability is just an inability of otherwise intelligent people — who may actually excel in other areas of performance — to learn certain selective tasks.

I believe that learning is limited when spontaneous and simultaneous access is not available to all of the following: the fastest electrical brain wave frequencies (beta) of the two-dimensional world, the slower brain wave frequencies (alpha) of the three-dimensional world, and the even slower brain wave frequencies (theta) of the state of "Oneness." [2]

Play detective with the following information, and see if you come to the same conclusion I have: all three realities are needed for optimal learning.

# TWO-DIMENSIONAL BETA

The two-dimensional world is associated with beta, the fastest frequencies of microvolts of electricity produced by our brains. Beta is defined as a rapid firing of electrical brain waves, 14 to 35+ times per second. The slower of the beta frequencies seem to be more helpful for learning new information, and rote memory. If these beta frequencies fire too rapidly, they can cause anxiety and be counterproductive to learning.

---

[2] Cade, C. Maxwell and Coxhead, Nona. *The Awakened Mind: Biofeedback and the Development of Higher States of Awareness.* London: Element Books, 1989. Research showing strong evidence for the importance of developing all brain wave frequencies across both hemispheres, rather than just learning to compensate.

***This two-dimensional/beta reality is responsible for:***

> habitual beliefs, rote memory, organizational skills
>
> verbal and written language
>
> active listening to language, and mental concentration
>
> storage of thousands of unrelated bits of information
>
> understanding the concept of time through clocks
>
> acceptance of rules without question
>
> acceptance of "facts" propounded by "experts"
>
> photographic memory for spelling, phone numbers, written text
>
> ability to recite memorized prose, poetry, jokes
>
> becoming a trivia expert, or "walking encyclopedia"
>
> high speed sequencing of movements (playing a musical instrument, speech, throwing darts)

***Too much beta, especially in the faster frequencies, without the balance of the slower alpha frequencies, is associated with:***

> performance anxiety and perfectionism
>
> concern over what others will think
>
> fear of spending time alone
>
> insomnia or inability to relax
>
> fragmented, hurried life
>
> need to talk all the time just to feel comfortable
>
> narrow black and white thinking
>
> slave to the clock and outdated rules
>
> critical of self and/or others
>
> learning disabilities related to the above traits

***Too little beta is associated with:***

> poor memory, especially for two dimensional input
>
> lack of motivation in the external world

unintentional irresponsibility to others

sense of mental dullness or fogginess

disorganization of thoughts and lack of organized routines

learning disabilities related to the above traits

# THREE-DIMENSIONAL ALPHA

The three-dimensional sensory world is associated with alpha brain wave frequencies. Alpha is defined as the microvolts of electricity discharged from the brain at a rate of 8 to 13 times per second. Children, advanced meditators, and highly creative people tend to produce the slower number of firings per second, while most adults produce the higher frequencies per second while in alpha.

***Three-dimensional/alpha reality is responsible for:***

seeing the world as three-dimensional in our inner vision

listening to music and pleasing sounds with appreciation

all sensory memories (fresh lemon on the tip of your tongue, colors from yesterday's sunset, friend's voice, the feel of velvet)

finding new solutions to old problems

unstructured creativity

taking in the world as it is, uninfluenced by others' verbal or written input

learning by doing, at one's own pace

spatial relations (perceiving 3-D objects in space from any angle, e.g., artists', engineers', and architects' perspectives)

being aware of multiple points of view in human relationships

awareness that rules are situational, and can be questioned

perspective and objectivity, resulting in fairness

an awareness of there being more to life than survival and daily routine

***Too much alpha, without the balance of the other frequencies, is associated with:***

untimely or unproductive daydreaming

poor survival skills, due to inadequate sense of healthy fear becoming detached from society's needs

not understanding the value of structure and routines

being unaware of time and scheduling responsibilities

being oblivious to one's importance in others' lives

living life only for one's own sensory pleasures

creativity that never amounts to anything externally productive

missed opportunities, wasted years

undisciplined mind, mindlessness, mental fog

learning disabilities related to the above traits

***Too little alpha is associated with:***

most of the anxiety problems associated with too much beta

blocked creative potential

lack of objectivity; poor problem-solving abilities

constant need for external stimulation to replace internal void

learning disabilities related to the above traits

# ONENESS IN THETA

Life before birth into three-dimensional reality was pure existence in the "Oneness" of our mothers' wombs. The predominant brain wave frequencies would have been theta, ranging from 4 to 7 electrical firings per second. Momentary interruptions of alpha (sensory perception) and beta (motor movement) responses to new or unexpected sounds or movements in our mothers' world would also occur. (Below 4 electrical firings per second, called delta, we are considered to be in deep sleep; but these slowest frequencies may yet reveal even greater mysteries.)

***The "Oneness state" of theta is associated with:***

deep, emotional feelings that remove our perception of detachment or separateness from others (including anger)

drowsiness, "twilight sleep" that occurs immediately before deep sleep; dreams, especially those of emotional content

a parent holding his or her newborn child

a child daydreaming about a puppy he wants his mother to buy him

a child missing her dad who no longer lives with her

a father feeling tremendous love and pride while imaging his adult child

altruism, the feeling of an "open heart"

advanced meditations of losing awareness of interpersonal boundaries

flashes of visions, insights, and other spontaneous gifts of creativity

profound spiritual experiences that leave one in a temporary state of bliss, with a sense of lacking nothing

### Too much theta, without the balance of the beta or alpha, is associated with:

rare advanced meditators (not necessarily desirable)

uncontrollable need for sleep

the extremely pleasant "aura" of transcendent radiance before a petite mal seizure in people susceptible to petite mal seizures

### Too little theta is associated with:

a detachment of feelings from daily living

an inability to feel love

a rejection of the need for integrating our "Oneness" experiences into our present lives

denial of our past "Oneness" bond with our mother

refusal to forgive our mothers for ending our "Oneness" reality with them

mistrust of others, including the people we say that we love

isolating ourselves from the purest forms of life: nature, animals, infants, and young children

need for excessive control of relationships

repulsion of primitive instincts, shown by inexplicable dislike or fear of animals

feeling superior or inferior to other people

# BRAIN WAVE FREQUENCIES, AND WHAT THEY MEAN[3]

| Electrical Firings Per Second | Frequency Range | Behavior/Skill |
|---|---|---|
| 35+ (High arousal) | high beta | performance anxiety |
| • | | conditioned fear |
| • | | reaction to real danger |
| • | beta | habitual beliefs |
| • | | verbal/written language |
| • | | rote memory |
| • | | organizational skills |
| • | | following arbitrary rules |
| • | | critical judgment |
| • | | productivity |
| • | alpha | sensory experiences |
| • | | sensory memories |
| • | | objective problem-solving |
| • | | creativity |
| • | theta | all strong feelings |
| • | | intimacy |
| • | | loss of social boundaries |
| • | delta | deep sleep |
| • | | the unknown |
| .05 Life/death Transition | | |

[3] Blundell, Geoffrey. *The Meaning of EEG*. London: Audio Limited, 26-28 Wendell Road, London W12 9RT; and Cade, Maxwell and Coxhead, Nona. "A New Way of Learning," *The Awakened Mind*. London: Element Books, 1989; and Danskin, David G. and Crow, Mark A. "EEG: Brain Wave Biofeedback Training," *Biofeedback: An Introduction and Guide*. Palo Alto, CA: Mayfield Publ. 1981; and Green, Elmer E., Green, Alyce E. *Beyond Biofeedback*, Ft. Wayne, Indiana: Knoll Publ., 1990.

## *Brain Frequencies and Creativity*

For a number of years now, writers who are not knowledgeable of brain functioning have been popularizing the idea that people are more left- or right-brained, and that right-brained people are more creative.

The truth is that the right brain doesn't really house any exclusive ability that is responsible for creativity.[4] There is a spot in the right hemisphere that is solely responsible for recognizing faces, and an area that helps us perceive spatial relationships between objects, whether they are presented two-dimensionally or three-dimensionally. However, neither of these functions is directly related to creative ability. A person can be as creative with their expression of words (left hemisphere) as they can be with the manipulation of objects in space (e.g., poets vs. architects).

The empirical evidence suggests that the main distinction between the left and right hemispheres is that the left hemisphere processes information through language, while the right hemisphere lacks the ability to process and communicate through language.[5] However, the right hemisphere is able to communicate the same information nonverbally, suggesting it is an aware, but silent partner to the left hemisphere. The popular speculation that the right hemisphere houses extraordinary abilities comes from a lack of understanding of how extraordinary our pre-language minds were in our early years. Without language biasing our beliefs, our natural common sense and sensory intuitions are impressive.

What these left-brain/right-brain armchair theorists have been talking about without knowing it, is the difference between the human abilities that relate to beta vs. alpha brain wave frequencies. Beta, which appears in both hemispheres, is present when cognitive functions involving language are employed. If speech is involved, including subvocalizing, beta will be more dominant in the left hemisphere over 95% of the time. Alpha is present in one or both hemispheres when creative problem-solving is occurring. When it is present in only one hemisphere, it is not always the same hemisphere. Where alpha manifests will depend on the task.

So, you see, we really can't say that beta and two-dimensional language are in the left hemisphere, and alpha and three-dimensional creativity are in the right hemisphere.

---

[4] Ornstein, Robert, and Thompson, Richard F. "The Divided Brain," *The Amazing Brain*. Boston: Houghton Mifflin, 1984.

[5] Corballis, Michael C. and Beale, Ivan L. "The Evolution of Symmetry and Asymmetry," *The Psychology of Left and Right*. Hillsdale, New Jersey: Lawrence Erlbaum, 1976.

The brain just doesn't work that way. When I do work with an individual who has a particular brain wave frequency limited to only one hemisphere, that person is always someone with a known learning disability.

This doesn't mean that all the literature out there on developing right brain creativity is useless. A lot of the exercises in those books are valid ways to develop the lower brain wave frequencies, especially in the alpha range.[6]

Optimal creativity comes from the use of all of your brain's abilities, represented by all frequencies. Remembering the "Oneness" + 2-D + 3-D formula will help you select the best programs and exercises to improve your creativity.

## *Brain Frequencies and the Arts*

Since the Arts are a common vehicle for the expression of our creativity they deserve special attention here, and can help clarify how all brain wave frequencies are needed to master any pursuit.

The necessity of theta is probably most easy to understand. All great creative expression is fueled by a passionate or intense level of emotion. When an artist doesn't feel this passion or intensity, the art form will only be a shadow of what it could have been.

Copying a drawing, or rehearsing dance steps, or practicing a musical composition are efforts to replicate creativity. However, when the basic copying of the drawing or the dance or the music is complete, there is always room for your own special interpretation of the art form to emerge in your finishing touches. It is the passionate emotion of theta that can make your interpretation of someone else's artistic creation, your own creative expression.

Alpha's part in artistic creativity is also probably pretty obvious. We create through our senses. Michelangelo and Leonardo da Vinci had a running debate as to which was the greater art, sculpture or painting. However, I think it is safe to say that there is no best way to express your creativity through your senses. All your senses, if well developed, can lead you to the joy of creativity.

---

[6] Edwards, Betty, *Drawing on the Right Side of the Brain.* Los Angeles: J.P. Tarcher, 1979; and Buzan, Tony. *Use Both Sides of Your Brain.* New York: E.P. Dutton, 1983; and Klauser, Henriette Anne, *Writing on Both Sides of the Brain.* San Francisco: Harper & Row, 1986; and Cherry, Clare; Godwin, Douglas and Staples, Jesse. *Is the Left Brain Always Right?* Belmont, CA: Fearon Teacher Aids, 1989. These are all excellent books for developing creativity, reflective of the lower brain wave frequencies in both hemispheres.

42

It is beta that people sometimes have difficulty connecting with creative expression. However, all the arts follow some structure. The musical scale, rules of proportion and shading in the visual arts, and choreographed dance, all rely on beta-generated rules.

Without beta rules and memory an artist can actually be handicapped. Imagine someone with a beautiful singing voice, full of theta feeling, and capable of near perfect pitch (alpha). If this person's language memory is poor, he or she will constantly be frustrated by the difficulty of memorizing lyrics, or the ability to recall them later. Instead this person may become a hummer or a whistler, never knowing the joy of developing his or her vocal creativity to the fullest.

The more a visual artist makes use of beta rules, the more likely it is that the art will accurately represent its three-dimensional counterpart in great detail. Some paintings, inspired by the visual beta realm, are hardly distinguishable from photographs.

In contrast, theta oriented artists may consider abstractions a greater form of art. These artists prefer to use as few beta rules as possible, trying to capture a theta experience in its purest form. This can never be totally accomplished; as soon as we desire to share our theta experience with others, we are forced into using some beta-generated form of communication or expression, in order to be understood by others. Theta emotion and alpha sensory experience need the form and structure that the beta realm can provide, in order to create a lasting impression of a creative moment in time.

Whether one learns music more visually, auditorily, or more through beta rules or theta experience shapes how music will be creatively expressed in our lives. It doesn't determine whether or not we will be talented. An extremely visual musician with strong beta capacity could excel in a busy orchestra where new sheet music is constantly being introduced. An extremely auditory musician with a strong connection to musical rhythms probably would not gravitate toward a structured expression of music requiring a great deal of sight reading. Rather, this person might do best as a soloist, or playing by ear, or improvising with other musicians who also relate to music primarily as an auditory experience at the alpha and theta levels. This would not mean that music in this case would not follow rules of structure, but that the rules may be out of their awareness. Many people who play a musical instrument by ear have no idea that they are following structured rules for musical composition; they just know it sounds right.

The many ways in which theta-emotion and beta-form interact with our various senses and motor capabilities give us an infinite variety of creative talent. The lovely thing about artistic expression is that there is no one way (or right way) to be creative.

## Brain Waves and Learning

Learning is limited when spontaneous and simultaneous access is not available to all of the following: the higher brain wave frequencies (beta) of the two-dimensional world, and the mid-range brain wave frequencies (alpha) of the three-dimensional world, and the lower brain wave frequencies (theta) of the state of "Oneness."

### ONENESS + 2-D + 3-D = OUR UNLIMITED POTENTIAL

| Developmental Stage of Life | "Lifetime" | Brain Waves |
|---|---|---|
| In Utero Experience | "Oneness" | theta |
| + Pre-Language Sensing | + "3D" | + alpha |
| + Post-Language Symbolism | + "2D" | + beta |
| = Full Life Experience | = Full Perceptual Awareness | = Whole Brain Functioning |
| | = Infinite Potential | |

There is nothing you will want to do with your life that cannot be improved by simultaneously drawing on the best of all three realities of existence, "Oneness," 3-D, and 2-D. Most people can see right away that the integration of 3-D and 2-D abilities is necessary for the natural process of learning.

Theta, however, is equally important for learning because it reflects our capacity for passion. Passion for knowledge and experience makes the difference between superficial dabbling in a subject, resulting in limited use of the information, and integrated absorption of the deepest meaning of the learning into all of our other personal understandings and life experiences. Being "one" with the new information allows us full power to creatively unfold that knowledge into new insights.[7]

---

[7] Only in the last few years has the importance of theta begun to be understood. In my first book (Sunbeck, Deborah T., *Infinity Walk: Preparing Your Mind to Learn,* Rochester, New York: Infinity Press, 1991, pp. 59-62), I spent a number of pages defending my findings that theta was essential to the learning process. However, since that time, researchers have been publishing their own findings on its usefulness.

Peniston, Eugene G. and Kulkosky, Paul J. "Alpha-Theta Brainwave Neuro-Feedback for Veterans with Combat-Related Post-Traumatic Stress Disorder," *Medical Psychotherapy,* 4, 1-14, 1991.

Boeving, Hugh. "Watching Addictions Disappear," *Menninger Perspective,* 1, 1993. (A theta biofeedback program for alcoholics)

 44

Optimally, we will mature as a species, to reflect our capacity for fully integrated minds that can spontaneously access all brain wave frequencies and their corresponding human abilities. Think of it: How wonderful it would be to have a world full of people who are intelligent, clear communicators, respectful of necessary social rules (beta traits); and have common sense, creativity, openness in their dealings with other people (alpha traits); and have a deep capacity to cherish all life on this planet (theta trait). What an incredible potential we have, as human beings!

***REFLECTIONS ON CHAPTER 4***
***ONENESS + 2-D + 3-D = OUR UNLIMITED POTENTIAL***

1.  List the beta qualities that come easily for you.
    List the beta qualities that you have yet to develop.

2.  List the alpha qualities that come easily for you.
    List the alpha qualities that you have yet to develop.

3.  List the theta qualities that come easily for you.
    List the theta qualities that you have yet to develop.

4.  List your ideas of how you could go about developing and refining your beta, alpha, and theta qualities.

# CHAPTER 5

# It Really Is All Yours for the Taking!

We have some very outstanding models for the success of our new formula for unlimited potential: Oneness + 2-D + 3-D. Albert Einstein's and Leonardo da Vinci's lives reflected this formula.

## ALBERT EINSTEIN (1879-1955)[1]

Einstein's brilliance went unnoticed during his youth. Knowing what you do now about the three realities we each live in, follow along with me through Einstein's youth. See if you come to the same conclusion that I have made: Einstein never prioritized two-dimensional reality over his earlier realities.

---

[1] Clayton, Lawrence, and Morrison, Jaydene. *Coping With a Learning Disability.* New York: Rosen Publishing Group, 1992, 105-106.

West, Thomas G. *In the Mind's Eye.* Buffalo, New York: Prometheus Books, 1991, 118-129.

Peare, Catherine Owens. *Albert Einstein: A Biography for Young People.* New York: Holt, 1949.

Bernstein, Jeremy. *Einstein.* New York: Viking Press, 1973.

Reef, Catherine. *Albert Einstein: Scientist of the 20th Century.* Minneapolis, Minn.: Dillon Press, 1991.

As a toddler, Einstein was slow to speak. Some reports say that he did not begin to speak until his second or third year. Even into his early teens, his lack of conversational skills gave him the appearance of having poor mastery over language. Einstein's comment on this was that he chose to not speak unless he felt correct in what he was saying. Later he found a language he felt very comfortable with, the unbiased language that seeks only the truth—the language of mathematical formulas.

From a very young age, Einstein was a quiet daydreamer. He preferred to wander off into nature contemplating questions that adults had no answers for, rather than to play organized games with other boys.

Einstein's childhood reaction to seeing a ceremonial parade of German soldiers marching in perfect unison was the opposite of most little boys. He became hysterical and could not be quieted down. Later he explained that he was scared by what appeared to be men who had lost their individual minds. This was an early sign that Einstein's mind took no socially accepted reality for granted. What he saw in those soldiers through his eyes was his own reality, and no amount of verbal explanation could convince him otherwise.

Some teachers found Einstein to be a disruptive force in school. One teacher complained that he found it very disturbing to see Einstein as a young boy, sitting in the back of the classroom with a smile on his face for no apparent reason. This teacher complained that Einstein's mysterious smiling violated the sense of respect every teacher deserves.

Another teacher reported that young Einstein was a source of embarrassment to him. Apparently, Einstein could be quite verbal when he was interested in an academic subject and wanted his questions answered. Einstein was reported to have been kept after school one day by a teacher who could no longer tolerate Einstein's constant barrage of unanswerable questions. Einstein was asked to no longer ask questions in class that did not have already established answers laid down in the textbook, because the teacher was feeling humiliated in front of the other children.

This teacher tried to explain to Einstein that the other children did not understand the difference between questions that no one had an answer for, and questions that a teacher was incompetent to answer. He asked Einstein to not humiliate him further. Whether Einstein was able to honor this request is not recorded in writings on his life.

Reports of Einstein's learning disabilities in the early school years appear to be somewhat inconsistent on the surface. He did poorly in anything that required written language and rote memory, but did exceptionally well in math. His overall grades were above average. Some writings on Einstein attribute his academic problems to his personality rather than to a learning problem. Einstein was fiercely independent, despised learning by rote, and found school to be a very unhappy experience.

The debate about whether a child's failures in school are caused by poor motivation or his or her brain's lack of readiness to master beta-related information is an unending one. Like the chicken and the egg riddle, whichever came first, it is perpetuated by the other. Whichever was true for Einstein, he himself wrote as a young man who had just dropped out of high school, that he believed himself to be lacking in imagination and practical ability!

With the help of friends, Einstein finally did receive a high school diploma through another school, and was accepted into a technical college. There friends helped him pass exams that were based on rote memory, through the loan of their detailed notes on class lectures.

Einstein was unsuccessful in finding a job after college. It is unclear if this was more because of his being a Jew during a time of prejudice, or because of his unremarkable academic records and unambitious personality. A college friend came to Einstein's rescue, and through a relative secured him a job as a technical clerk for the Patent Office.

Einstein later said that his years at the Patent Office were the happiest in his life. Though a poorly paid position with no status, it allowed him the freedom and privacy to think about his evolving theories during the work day, with energy left in the evening to continue his mental calculations and to be with his young family. Even after Einstein became famous for the theories he formulated while working his civil service job, he showed no particular interest in money or social status.

Einstein's healthy blend of beta and alpha capacities should be apparent by now, but what about his capacity for theta? Einstein came from a warm, nurturing family and was close to both his mother and father. He deeply loved his only sibling, a younger sister nicknamed Maja, and they remained lifelong, emotionally supportive companions.

Those who knew Einstein were also aware of a spiritual, or perhaps mystical, depth to his being. Einstein spent the second half of his life working on his unified field theory, which he hoped would tie all natural laws of life and the universe together into one integrated explanation. Perhaps we can say that Einstein was searching for the mathematical formula that would explain the "Oneness" of the universe.

Einstein thrived in nature and in the company of good friends who understood and appreciated his unique mind. The very devotion of his loyal, life-long friends speaks to his capacity for profound human closeness, which is reflective of theta.

Though we don't have any record of Einstein's brain being assessed for all brain wave frequencies, we do have some information about his brain based on EEG findings. Einstein is reported to have generated high voltage alpha brain waves, along with beta brain waves, while computing math problems that others might try to solve by beta alone. He never missed an opportunity for a new creative insight. Einstein's life and creative gifts to the world are truly a wonderful example of the Oneness + 2-D + 3-D formula at work.

# LEONARDO DA VINCI (1452-1519)[2]

Leonardo da Vinci is considered by many to be the most versatile genius who ever lived. His artistic masterpieces such as the Mona Lisa and The Last Supper led some to know of him as an artist, but Leonardo excelled in every subject that caught his interest. His mastery of the relationship between 2-dimensional painting and the 3-dimensional life that his paintings represented led to expertise in botany, zoology, biology, geology, anatomy, architecture, and engineering.

Leonardo was as much an inventor as an artist. Some of his designs included indoor plumbing, the first workable parachute, military devices and weapons, palaces, canal systems, prefabricated houses (used for hunting trips), the first self-propelled vehicle, a precursor to the first airplane, pre-planned designs for modern cities, and a military ship that could move under water.

[2] Corballis, Michael C., and Beale, Ivan L. *The Psychology of Left and Right.* Hillsdale, New Jersey: Lawrence Erlbaum, 1976, 178-180.

West, Thomas G. *In the Mind's Eye.* Buffalo, New York: Prometheus Books, 1991, 145-147.

Lerman, Leo. *Leonardo da Vinci: Artist and Scientist.* New York: Bobbs-Merrill, 1940.

Friedenthal, Richard. *Leonardo da Vinci: A Pictorial Biography.* New York: Viking Press, 1959.

Noble, Iris, *Leonardo da Vinci: the Universal Genius.* New York: Norton, 1965.

Venezia, Mike, *Da Vinci.* Chicago: Children's Press, 1988.

Everything in Leonardo's life stemmed from his own creativity. For instance, he wrote his own songs, complete with verses, and played them on a sliver lute that he designed. The lute was shaped to represent a horse's head, with the teeth serving as the frets that created the different tones. The lute was so admired by others that it won him an important commission by a wealthy man who wanted to own the instrument.

If Leonardo was known to be a frustrated or unhappy person, his torment would have stemmed from the constant need to subjugate his creative inspiration to the whims of wealthy people who paid for his services. Many of his unfinished masterpieces were put aside because he had to work on projects that his patrons demanded of him. When he was left alone to create, he was fulfilled.

Leonardo also experienced the loneliness that comes from not having peers who could match his intellect and creativity. Instead he turned to the world of his inner thoughts, and carried a notebook with him everywhere he went. He left the world 5,000 written pages of insights, inventions, theories, and philosophy that are still proving useful today. One sentence in his notes that caught my attention was, "It is not enough to believe what you see, you must also understand what you see." On keeping a notebook he said, "Consult Nature in everything and write it all down. Whoever thinks he can remember the infinite teachings of Nature flatters himself. Memory is not that huge."

Like Einstein's, Leonardo's brain also refused to sacrifice his three-dimensional perspective to two-dimensional reality. How can we know this, given that he lived before the age of electronic brain wave technology? He left us with some very big clues.

## CLUE #1

Many of Leonardo's volumes of personal written notes are in mirror image writing, read from right to left.

*His handwriting would look like this. (\*reversed\*)*

Leonardo didn't have to write this way. He was quite capable of writing like everyone else. However, he was left-handed, and that made right to left writing easier and faster for him. And, since he had no difficulty viewing letters as three-dimensional objects, it didn't matter to him which angle he would write or read them from.

## CLUE #2

Leonardo also had little respect for the rules of written language, and placed words on a page sometimes in ways that only he could decipher. He would freely make up words or interchange their meanings. He was very poor at spelling, grammar, and sentence structure, and his mirror-imaged notes would sometimes give the appearance of a secret Morse code or a clever riddle.

## CLUE #3

Leonardo showed signs of transcending the barriers of three-dimensional reality into "Oneness" in some of his religious paintings. His most sacred images of Jesus, saints, and angels are considered masterpieces in their transcendence of the biological duality that is created in humans through the two genders of male and female. His brush depicted the qualities of God as the perfected balance of male and female qualities. Because of this, it is impossible to determine the gender of the subject in many of his paintings of spiritual beings.

Unfortunately, unlike Einstein, Leonardo was apparently not able to find this Oneness outside of his work. He wrote, "Alone, you belong to yourself only; with even one other person you are only half yourself, and you will be less and less yourself in proportion to the number of companions."

# MY VERY DYNAMIC MORNING

Can we hope to develop our brains to the levels of these men? If we can, I believe it will be through utilizing the Oneness + 2-D + 3-D formula. This formula represents a potential for everyone, not just for a few special people. To give you a better idea of how this formula can influence our brain wave patterns I measured the frequencies and magnitude (power) of my own brain waves at three different points during a typical morning of writing this book. Follow along with me through my morning.

**7 AM.** I have a light breakfast. Since eating a large meal or consuming sugar or caffeine products will alter my brain response I avoid them. Afterwards, I decide to walk through the field behind my home before heading for the computer. My dogs take off, running in front of me, chasing each other through the high grass. The sunrise peeking over the top of the woods at the far end of the field seems especially beautiful today. The dogs catch my attention and talk me into five minutes of frisbee throwing before we return to the house.

After hooking myself up to one of my brain wave machines (EEG), and quieting myself awhile to get an accurate reading on the equipment, my current brain pattern begins to emerge.[3]

As you can see in Graph #1, the left side of my brain looks more active at the moment. When comparing the beta in my left hemisphere to my right hemisphere beta there is a considerable difference in the magnitude of the electrical voltage being generated. Does this tell me I am more left brained, or left brain dominant? No, it just tells me that my language center is housed in the left hemisphere, as is true for over 95% of all people.[4] Beta is always active when cognitive processes are present.

Left brain     Right brain

beta                                     beta

alpha                                     alpha

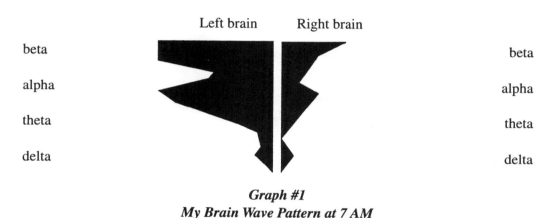

theta                                     theta

delta                                     delta

*Graph #1*
*My Brain Wave Pattern at 7 AM*

Looking down to the alpha range I see mine is peaking around 11.5 cycles per second in both hemispheres but is a little stronger in the left. This is normal for adults at rest. Children and adults engaged in very creative projects will show a lower alpha peak. There is virtually no theta present at the moment. This overall brain wave pattern is a very typical one for normal adults when their brains are on "idle."

Once I have all this pre-test information recorded, I move on to start a new chapter of the book. The EEG electrodes that I attached to my scalp in order to record the microvolts of electricity generated by my brain are kept in place, so I can quickly record new readings throughout the morning.

---

[3] The particular equipment I used that morning was a visual display electroencephalography (EEG) that shows left and right brain readings separately across 14 frequency bands ranging from .75 - 38 Hz. (electrical firings per second).

[4] Benson, D. Frank. "Language in the Left Hemisphere," in Benson, D. Frank and Zaidel, Eran. (Ed.) *The Dual Brain: Hemispheric Specialization in Humans.* New York: The Guilford Press, 1985.

**9 AM.** After an hour of composing directly into the computer I decide to take a break and check my brain wave pattern again. Graph #2 shows that a very different pattern has emerged. There are three notable changes. First, the overall magnitude or power of my brain's electrical voltage has greatly increased. Second, I'm very aware of the increased symmetry between the right and left sides of my brain. They are both pulling their own weight, and fully cooperating. The large amounts of beta and alpha waves reflect that the last hour spent on writing this book has been both very productive (beta) and creative (alpha) for me. This was my exact feeling of how the writing was coming along during the hour. I can always tell when I'm operating from greater brain potential rather than struggling with imbalances in brain wave frequencies and magnitudes between hemispheres. Some of us call this "having a good day" versus "having a bad day." The third noticeable difference is that even though I am more awake than my first reading at 7 am, I am actually showing a little *more* theta.[5]

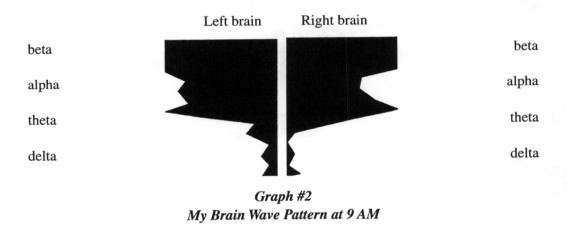

Left brain　　　Right brain

beta　　　　　　　　　　　　　　　　beta

alpha　　　　　　　　　　　　　　　alpha

theta　　　　　　　　　　　　　　　theta

delta　　　　　　　　　　　　　　　delta

*Graph #2*
*My Brain Wave Pattern at 9 AM*

Since I'm far from being asleep, I have to conclude that the increased theta is reflecting my creative process unfolding from the Oneness that lives in the rich unconscious. Since my beta and alpha frequencies are fully active, I am finding it easy to allow formerly unconscious insights to integrate into my waking consciousness and out my fingers into the computer. Back to the book.

---

[5] For more information on theta, read Green, Elmer E. & Green, Alyce E. *Beyond Biofeedback,* Ft. Wayne, Indiana: Knoll Publishing, 1990; Mavromatis, Andreas, *Hypnagogia: The Unique State of Consciousness Between Wakefulness and Sleep,* NY: Rutledge Publications, 1991.

**10:30 AM.** I take a second break, this time to relax from the beginning of eye tension caused by the computer screen. The Infinity Walk sensorimotor pattern, explained in Part III of this book, is great for relieving eye strain. So, I decide to do a little experiment. Infinity Walk is an exercise that coordinates sensory and motor functioning between the two sides of the brain and body. For my little experiment I decide to do Infinity Walk while listening to a recording of a full orchestra performing Mozart.[6] This alone would be enough to give me an incredible surge of enthusiasm, but I decide to add an affirmation I have created that I know opens my theta frequencies. You are welcome to use it as your own if it feels right for you. This is it:

> *I do not blindly accept man made reality*[7]
> *I seek the natural laws of life*
> *My spirit thrives on the truth beyond relative reality*

As I say these three lines out loud, over and over again, while doing Infinity Walk, I think about how I don't need to consciously know all natural universal laws in order to accept them fully into me; scientists are still discovering them. I tell myself I don't need to consciously understand all that is beyond the relative two-and three-dimensional realms, because this message is for my unconscious mind that is intimate with the Oneness.

I have gained increasing faith in this affirmation because the words activate my theta, a realm in me that knows more than my conscious self. There is a peaceful emotion that emerges in me when my theta is activated. It is an emotion I equate with deep Truth.

If the meaning of my affirmation doesn't make sense to you, then it would be better to create your own. You don't need a sophisticated brain wave analyzer to know when you have created just the right affirmation for yourself. Your body will tell you. My body and brain tingle within five minutes, and I experience a sense of lightness, joy, and sometimes even feel my heart giggling!

---

[6] The value of certain types of music for changing brain wave frequencies, states of consciousness, and helping to integrate the whole brain has been researched. Read: Campbell, Don G, *Introduction to the Musical Brain,* St. Louis, Missouri: MMB Music, 1986; and Halpern, Steven, *Tuning the Human Instrument,* Belmont, CA: Spectrum Research Institute, 1980.

[7] I use "man made" because most of our social and cultural habits that I find myself questioning were developed during a time in history when men were solely in power. The use of this term is not meant as a slight to men or women, but helps me reflect more deeply on how long a culture can hold to unhealthy or insensitive practices, when they become habitual (beta) to both male and female citizens.

Left brain    Right brain

beta                                                        beta

alpha                                                       alpha

theta                                                       theta

delta                                                       delta

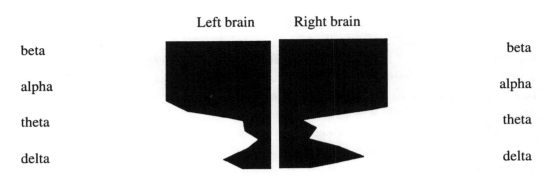

*Graph #3*
*My Brain Wave Pattern at 10:30 AM*

I decide to take a brain wave reading after doing all of the above, for five minutes. Subjectively, I feel both very awake and in a pleasant calm state. I feel like I am bubbling with life and totally at peace at the same time. I have a sense that my fingers could never type fast enough to get all the creative thoughts that are floating up to consciousness onto the computer. I feel very full and very complete.

I am no more or no less of an Einstein or a Leonardo da Vinci than you are. Anyone, under the right circumstances, can operate from their vast human potential, too great to even define or fully understand. Einstein did not think he was unusually imaginative. Leonardo disliked people calling him creative. They were both simply doing what came naturally for them. We can do the same.

### REFLECTIONS ON CHAPTER 5
### IT REALLY IS ALL YOURS FOR THE TAKING!

1.  List your memories of peak moments in your life, when all of your being seemed to be working in perfect harmony, and you found whatever you were doing to be amazingly more easy than you expected it to be. Is there any reason to believe that you could not produce such experiences at will, if you knew how?

---

C H A P T E R   6

---

# My Two Childhoods

Like many of you, I also struggled through the adjustment to two-dimensional reality during my early childhood. My inner battle to hold on to what I felt to be intuitively true, against all the verbal onslaught of "facts" and rules, is still very clear in my mind. That struggle created two distinct but parallel childhoods for me — my inner world life, and my life in society.

I ruled my inner mystical world of the lower brain wave frequencies. I was ruled *by* all those in power over me in my outer life of beta-reality. The distinction was clear to me; so was my choice of which I preferred at that time.

The following two brief stories reflect my two childhoods. They are written from my perspective as a child, as I remember them to be.

## CHILDHOOD #1

### *Headlines! Four Foot Tall Social Scientist Struggles to Understand Human Language!*

I was a learning handicapped child.
So much so, that my mom says
        dad had been quite concerned my first years
that I might be mildly retarded.
He never showed it.

Mom just says I was a good baby, easy delivery, never cried, slept well through the night, wasn't fussy.

I didn't need to be entertained like the others, and since I showed little interest in exploring my environment once I could move about, she didn't have to watch me as carefully.

Mom says she never thought I was retarded, just that I was a quiet child,

*DIFFERENT FROM THE OTHERS.*

The first time I realized that there was something
**WRONG**
about the way I was
**DIFFERENT,**
was in first grade.

We were being introduced to written language,
and I just wasn't getting it.

Every week grew worse, as more words were added to the
stories, I couldn't keep track of them all.

I remember fleeting feelings of
quiet embarassment,
My head down over the book,
so the teacher wouldn't notice.

The other children were actually understanding all this stuff.
They were waving their arms in the air,

**hoping** they would be called on to read.

I WAS TOTALLY STUMPED.

Things just kept getting worse. I couldn't remember spelling words like the
other children,

I couldn't recite the answers to the catechism questions in religion class. The words I
thought I had memorized, just disappeared when I was called on.

Sometimes I'd have the answer in my head, or thought I did, but when I was ready to
raise my hand,

I couldn't
get my tongue to move fast enough to form the words.

Rather than sound funny, I'd say nothing at all.

I didn't know it at the time, but Dad had been a slow reader, and had stuttered until his
late teens. If I had tried to force it, I probably would have too.

Eventually, I learned how to avoid being called on, a
very important
**survival**
talent in such situations.

Besides, by the time I could find the word I was thinking of, and formulate its
pronunciation,

*A CONVERSATION WOULD HAVE PASSED ME BY.~~~*

That didn't really bother me, I never much wanted to talk to people. I
**liked**
**listening.**

Well, actually, it bothered me sometimes, but only when someone would
speak
for me, saying,

**"Oh, she doesn't talk, she's shy."**

I wanted to say

# I'M NOT SHY!

But I didn't, because then I would have to talk.

I did love school though, because

**I loved to learn,** not by reading, but by
listening to every word a teacher said.

**I loved** to hear about anything new.

My intense listening is probably what saved me from ever failing a grade.

My lowest point in grade school was the weekend I attempted to learn
the MULTIPLICATION TABLE.

The other students were already reciting it in class.

How did they do it?

I had had enough!

I was determined to find the answer to this mystery.
Determined to prove to myself that if they could do it,
I could do it too.

I armed myself with my arithmetic book, and

locked myself away in my bedroom.

If someone came to my door, I'd just call out

*"I'm studying."*

*"Deborah's studying?"*

Then I'd hear one of my parents say

# *"Leave Deborah alone, she's studying."*

This must of been my first real attempt at studying, because I don't ever before remember such royal treatment!

I was relieved of all my household chores that weekend, and even allowed to leave the table as soon as I'd finished eating,

a rule that was never broken before at our family table.

I'd rush back to my bedroom, to test myself;
how many did I remember?

Did I
*lose any numbers* while eating?

I knew all the times 1, and I could remember the times 2,

I would just add the number twice, I could do that right in my head.

Times 5 and times 10 were easy because of nickels and dimes. I just thought of money and I knew the answer right away.

But **NO!** No, I had forgotten the other ones.

Exhaustion would sweep over me each time I'd realize I still hadn't figured it out, the secret to the multiplication table.

Wait, wait! 9 x 9 = 81, and 81 is 8+1 = 9. **Maybe that's it!**

Let's try. 4 x 4 = 16; 16 would be 1 + 6 = 7?
No, that didn't work at all.

I still didn't have it.

I'd glance out at my *beloved outdoors*; it was calling me, but I couldn't go.

I WOULDN'T LET MYSELF.

So, I'd take another short nap, thinking, maybe I'll figure it out when I
WAKE UP.

But I never did. I never did figure out that multiplication table.

I never read a single textbook either.

Not that I didn't try.

Every September I'd carry my new set of books home from school, with a
*fresh*
*determination.*

YES, this year would be different. This year I would

## READ THESE BOOKS.

I wanted to know what was in them. My mind
ACHED to learn.

I was *curious*
about everything, always
*wondering.*

# YES

I WAS GOING TO READ THESE BOOKS, I WAS GOING TO START

**RIGHT THIS MINUTE.**

# TAKING THE PLEDGE
over the books, as if I was standing in the courtroom with

my hand on a Bible,
I'd sit down and begin my new school year of
homework.

And each year, just like the years before, I'd only get a couple of paragraphs
into the first page of the first book, before my mind would start
SINKING INTO A DAZE.

THREATENING to rapidly plunge me into a

# NARCOLEPTIC COMA

if I didn't stop IMMEDIATELY!

— if I didn't immediately stop trying to comprehend a line of text that my
eyes had scanned for the UMPTEENTH time.

It was just as well.
I had already forgotten the first paragraph.

I'd leave my books, and go for a walk down the street, to
*my favorite place*
in Ellision Park,

a place, up on a hill,
where I could
sit,
and sing

and wonder about things.

Michael D-luca
94

# CHILDHOOD #2

*Headlines!*
*Four Foot Tall Singing Mystic Refuses to Talk!*

We grew up next to Ellision Park.

Every day that I could, I would find some time to

*quietly* slip away from the house, to make my
*private pilgrimage* to the

top of the hill in the center of the park.

This particular hilltop was accessible only by foot trails through the
**SACRED WOODS.**

I knew it was *sacred* because of how *gently* my dad would walk
through it when we all came down to the park together.

It was the exact same way he would walk as he entered our church
on Sundays.

We were usually late for church, so we'd all be rushing from the
car to get to the church door,

But when dad went through that church door, his walk would
change, just like when he would

~ step into the woods.

Woods are strange like that.
You can't see the *door*,
but it's always there,

a place where one step makes the difference between standing on
*sacred ground*,
or being outside the woods.

I could tell dad knew exactly where the *door to the woods* was,
because his walk always changed then.

*I could feel it too.*

Understanding all this, I would be especially quiet moving up the
trail, on my daily *pilgrimage*,

stepping over any *new seedlings* trying to take root on the worn path.

I could sense the trees watching me, and when I was particularly
careful to not disturb any new growth, they would thank me, by
rustling their leaves.

I would keep myself from laughing when they did this, just like you're not
supposed to
laugh in church,

but I knew they could see my BIG SMILE.

They knew how much I loved it, when they would wave their rustling leaves at me.

As I reached the top of the hill, I would continue on
immediately to my destination,

*careful* to leave the rest of the hill *undisturbed*,

so I would be **welcomed** back.

My destination was a little perch I had made on the edge of the
steepest section of the hilltop, my favorite secret place.

There, I would begin my daily ritual of singing, very *quietly*
though, so no one down below could hear.

Each day, I would look forward to a particular feeling that
singing would produce in my head and chest.

I didn't have a word for that feeling then, but today I know it as

## *PASSION.*

Feeling the vibrations from my voice resonating inside my skull,
is in fact my first memory of experiencing

trance induced
***ecstasy.***

By modulating the sounds coming from my throat, I could change
the vibrations inside my brain, and with it produce moment to moment

changes in mood,
and perception.

I had a song for everyone, the trees, the clouds, the wind.
I created special songs for each chipmunk too.

Squirrels were always too busy to visit for very long, but the
chipmunks seemed to have plenty of time.

They were special in how they would sit up on their hind legs and
listen to me sing my song to them. Never running off before I was done.

Chipmunks are especially polite animals that way.

I wouldn't always sing though.

Sometimes, I would be very still up on that hill, and
listen to *nature sing her song* to the world.

Nature is always singing, and seeing that I also loved to sing,
this seemed to make us *especially close.*

I also did a lot of wondering about things up on that hill. But,
I was particular about what I'd wonder.

I only thought about things that
**no one had any answers for,**
even if they
***pretended*** they did,

about things like
***God,***

or what happens when you
die.

Sometimes I'd sit up on that hill planning things. Like new ways
to make my cat or dog
*fall asleep.*

I was fascinated with the process of falling asleep. I'd watch
myself go through the stages of sleep induction every night.

By hanging in there as long as possible before losing consciousness,
I found that I could choose my own dreams, rather than dreaming whatever

happened to be playing that night.

I loved to dream, but especially when I could make them
*anything I wanted them to be.*

All that sleep practicing on my cat and dog really came in handy
when I started baby-sitting.

Everyone in the neighborhood wanted me as their baby-sitter. I could get their kids to quiet down and fall asleep in minutes.

But, I have to say though,

that my favorite thing to do up on that hill in Ellision park, was to

# SING.

Sometimes I'd even be successful in merging my sound, my vibration, in exact synchrony with nature's.

# This was the ultimate.

This would send my brain
**soaring to such heights of ecstasy,**
that *tears*
would be pushed right out of my eyes,

as a *shiver*
deep inside me

would escape *up my spine.*

In my child's mind,

I knew, with the absolute knowingness
that only a *naive child* can know,

that I was, in that moment,

as close to GOD,
as a person was allowed to be.


If circumstances had allowed me to live only one of my two childhood lives, I would have chosen to live my second story. A non-verbal mystical existence was much more appealing to me than the world of adults. Other children might have chosen the constant struggle to fit into their social structure. Both choices have their own kinds of rewards.

*Enjoying All Realities:  Oneness + 2-D + 3-D*

Fortunately, I never had to make that choice. So, the "Oneness" + 2-D + 3-D formula was able to develop more naturally in me, than for some.

However, I also did not have this owner's manual while growing up, so I didn't know I was progressing along as well as I was. I had doubts about my intelligence, just as Einstein and hundreds of other "learning handicapped" people have learned to doubt themselves.

Looking back over my own history of learning, I remember my struggles to learn two-dimensional language symbols at the same speed my peers were mastering these written words and sentences. When I bring back these memories, something deep in me feels gratitude toward my brain for not letting my young mind master language so well that two-dimensional thinking might have become master over me later in life.

It is quite possible, as some research studies suggest, that children who give up alpha, and increase beta when they read, do better academically in the early grades.[1] Beta represents cognitive memory, which is all that is needed for most early academic success. Alpha represents sensory memory, and may get in the way when first learning to read. A mind that wants to live the story through three-dimensional sensory involvement, as the words are being read, may get in the way of word recognition. My brain never gave up alpha participation in anything I did, and reading did come slowly for me.

However, when my two-dimensional abilities finally caught up with me in my twenties, the result was a capacity to devour books in one sitting. When I read now, I enter into the three-dimensional reality of what I am reading, just as I used to enter pictures as a young child. I live the sentences; later I remember not the words, but the experiences. As I live what I read, I simultaneously apply all that I am experiencing to all that I remember experiencing from the past. Out of this comes new insights. I can hardly pick up a newspaper without triggering a new idea. I don't know if I ever would have enjoyed reading as a catalyst for creativity if I had given up alpha as a young reader.

The other side of this is that I still misspell words, and reverse letters and words on occasion. Only now, there is no negative connotation attached to these "variations" from beta rules on language. In fact, the more I find myself reversing written symbols, the more the content of what I am writing seems to be creative or insightful. What used to be a source of embarrassment is now just an indicator that I have entered into my ideas so completely that I have temporally lost contact with the beta rules of two-dimensional language structure.

## Famous People with Learning Problems

If you have had specific difficulties in learning, then add your name to the following list.

| | |
|---|---|
| ALBERT EINSTEIN | thought to be "dull" in early years due to extremely poor rote memory; slow to speak. |
| LEONARDO DA VINCI | dyslexic and a mirror-image writer; poor at spelling, grammar, sentence structure |
| HANS CHRISTIAN ANDERSON | dyscalculia (math disability)[2] |

---

[1] Lubar, Joel F. "Electroencephalographic Biofeedback and Neurological Applications," in Basmajian, John V. (Ed.) *Biofeedback: Principles and Practice for Clinicians.* 2nd edition, Baltimore: Williams & Wilkins, 1983.

LUDWIG VAN BEETHOVEN      dyslexic and attention-deficit[3]

THOMAS EDISON            "My father thought I was stupid,[4] and I almost decided I must be a dunce." "—always at the foot of the class."

LOUIS PASTEUR            dyslexic and dysgraphic (written reversals)[5]

WINSTON CHURCHILL        repeated a class in English three times; forced to walk at end of student line due to having lowest grade in class[6]

GEORGE PATTON            dyslexic[7]

WILLIAM BUTLER YEATS     severe dyslexia: "—the subtile and origonality of these vigerus Keltic letters shows such scholorship as to leave the reader fealing decideldy exausted" (quote from personal letter written by Yeats)[8]

_____

(write your name here)

### REFLECTION ON CHAPTER 6
### MY TWO CHILDHOODS

1.  Write the story (stories) of your own childhood. Be sure to include all the wonderful insights your young mind had about people, life, family, school, nature, life's mysteries, etc.

_____

[2] Clayton, Lawrence, and Morrison, Jaydene. *Coping With a Learning Disability.* New York: Rosen Publishing Group, 1992.

[3] Ibid. 107-108

[4] Ibid. 106-107; and, West, Thomas, G. *In the Mind's Eye.* Buffalo, New York: Prometheus Books, 1991, 137-141.

[5] Clayton, Lawrence, and Morrison, Jaydene, Ibid. 108-109.

[6] West, Thomas G. *In the Mind's Eye.* Buffalo, New York: Prometheus Books, 1991, 149-166.

[7] Ibid. 166-168.
Clayton, Lawrence, and Morrison, Jaydene. *Coping With a Learning Disability.* New York: Rosen Publishing Group, 1992, 104-105.

[8] West, Thomas G. *In the Mind's Eye.* Buffalo, New York: Prometheus Books, 1991, 168-175.

---
## PART 2
---

# Roadblocks
# and
# Closed Paths

WALK  
THE        THE  
INFINITY        INFINITY  
WALK        WALK  
YES        YES  
ACT        ACT  
TO        TO  
GO      GO  
TO  TO  
O  
TO  TO  
GO      GO  
TO        TO  
ACT        ACT  
YES        YES  
WALK        WALK  
INFINITY        INFINITY  
THE        THE  
WALK  

PAMELA GOOD

CHAPTER 7

# What's Happening When You Can't Learn? A Look At Brain Waves

$\mathbf{T}$*here are six types of learning restrictions that can occur when the Oneness + 2-D + 3-D formula is not present in our thoughts and actions.*

*These are:*

1. *Anxiety*: Strong presence of high frequency beta, with little alpha, and absence of positively generated theta

2. *Trance*: Presence of alpha and/or theta, with little beta in one or both hemispheres, except when talking or moving

3. *Last Minute Panic*: Alternation between Trance as preferred internal state, and uncontrollable Anxiety under testing or deadline conditions

4. *Weak Links*: Relatively little activity is present at any frequency, or consistently diminished activity at higher frequencies across both hemispheres. May suggest a neurochemical weakness at the sites of electrical firing in the brain. This brain wave pattern has responded to nutrition and drug therapy (e.g., Ritalin)

5.  *Chaos:*         Undisciplined mind: Strong frequencies of beta, alpha, and theta are available, but emotional issues unrelated to learning prevent the mind from focusing on the task long enough to create a successful experience (Much more rare: possible chemical/hormonal imbalance, or medical problem causing the emotional instability)

6.  *Blocked Theta:*    Beta and alpha may be active, and there may be an absence of any obvious academic learning problems. The ongoing absence of day time theta represents blocked capacity to love ourselves or others, greatly restricting our capacities to involve ourselves fully in life

Let's turn to these six categories in real students and adults, so that their meanings can come alive for you.

## *"Anxious Ann"*

Ann was a precocious preschooler. Adults were charmed by her ability to carry on clever conversations. Her parents were delighted when she showed an interest in reading at age four and a half, and did everything they could to encourage her reading abilities.

Ann was the perfect student. She set her goal at getting A's in all academic subjects, and would be upset when she didn't get one, vowing to herself that she would study even harder in the future. She was uncoordinated in gym class, showed minimal art talent, but could carry enough of a tune to be in chorus. It bothered her that she was never given a solo; she didn't realize it, but sometimes her pitch was off. Not always getting A's in these non-academic subjects didn't worry her. She knew that they were not as valued as the ones she did well in.

Teachers often chose her to head up class projects. Ann was a great organizer, and a natural take-charge person. Students seemed to like her well enough when she was organizing their projects, but she was far from what you would call a popular student. She always thought it was because students were jealous of her, but it was really because she never gave anyone else a chance to talk.

No one realized it then, but Ann was uncomfortable with silence. She didn't mean to offend the other students, but she needed to be hearing or speaking words constantly. So, if no one else was talking, she would take the responsibility for keeping the silence away by producing constant verbal chatter.

Underneath Ann's incredible academic competence and leadership abilities was a very nervous person. She panicked the night before every big exam, cramming every fact and figure she could into her head. It only took one mistake to spoil a perfect 100% on an exam, and she wanted that perfect score.

Getting a perfect score wasn't as easy for Ann as you might think. She had trained her mind to memorize countless facts (beta) needed for languages and history, but had neglected her natural abilities to problem-solve three-dimensional information (alpha), needed for math and the sciences. She didn't realize this; no one had ever told her that there is more to intelligence than reading and memorization.

That was really too bad, because Ann would have done anything to get others' respect and admiration, even keep her natural three-dimensional perspective of life.

Ann also panicked in social situations outside of school. If she couldn't be in charge of the social event, she didn't know what to do with herself. She could hardly wear her report card on her blouse, and her academic successes had become her entire identity. She felt empty and scared without her "A student" label.

Ann buried herself in books throughout college, and was offered a prestigious executive position in a top corporation immediately on graduating from college. She dated a number of young men during her college years but never really fell in love.

Worried that she was falling behind her peers in getting married by a "respectable age," she decide to marry a young executive at her corporate firm. She based her selection of him on his intelligence, good looks, and status with the company. Their marriage lasted two years, before they mutually decided to end it. Instead of their daily proximity leading to love, they just found one another to be increasingly irritating to be with.

Ann's life hasn't changed much since her early school years. She still panics when she gives herself a moment to feel that sense of emptiness and inadequacy that she hides so well, deep inside her. She still takes charge of every organization she involves herself in, and there have been many of those. Ann keeps her spare time so full of admirable community work that most people don't even notice her loneliness.

*Comment: A person does not have to be an A-student in school to be an "Anxious Ann." Anyone who values beta-type successes more than enjoying daily living in our three-dimensional world is going to experience frequent stress and feelings of in-security or emptiness.*

## "Trancing Timmy"

Timmy had been a very happy preschooler. He loved to play outdoors, and could entertain himself for hours with fantasy friends. His parents had appreciated that he was such an easy-going child, but all that changed when school started.

Timmy had been held back a year in kindergarten because he lacked pre-reading skills and "maturity." He was held back another year in second grade because of not progressing in reading. He was finally put in a special class, along with other slow learners.

Timmy didn't get a lot of sympathy for his reading difficulties. Teachers labeled him an unmotivated daydreamer. They might have been kinder if he showed poor abilities in all subjects, but Timmy did exceptionally well in all the hands-on science projects and was starting to show a little progress in math. Once they could see that he could comprehend subjects he showed an interest in, they came down harder on him in reading class. "Timmy, stop looking out the window! Pay attention! Sit up straight! Hold your book properly!"

Timmy never seemed overly embarrassed about his predicament, even when other children teased him. Not that it didn't bother him, he just didn't stay out of his fantasies long enough to worry about it. In some ways, it was hard to not like Timmy. He never seemed to lose his childhood innocence.

Timmy was often a topic at teachers' conferences. How should they handle his tardiness for class, his forgetting to bring his books to school, forgetting to take his homework home, and so on? They could feel him slip away into his fantasy world any time they talked to him about his countless memory lapses. Timmy would look at them with his big round eyes, his face glowing with tranquillity, and they would know immediately that his mind was elsewhere, somewhere they did not have access to.

After he graduated from high school, Timmy's parents helped him get a job doing assembly line work at a local factory. He was such a likable person that it took no time at all before a young lady at the factory, named Mary, started planning the rest of his life for him. They fell in love, married, and bought a little run-down farm house on the edge of town. Mary quit work after their second child, and took charge of budgeting their expenses so they could get by on less and less money as each new child arrived.

People driving by Timmy and Mary's place look over the happy home with a critical two-dimensional eye. They see an old building they wouldn't feel safe walking into, and more children and animals than any reasonable person would try to support. They see all kinds of things they disagree with, but they can't feel what Timmy and Mary have. Tim and Mary have love.

Timmy has continued to enjoy his factory job because it gives him plenty of time to think and dream. He's also very proud of his wife and growing family, and his ability to support them.

The old farm house is also slowly taking shape. It turned out that Timmy has a natural ability for carpentry, plumbing, electrical work, and auto repair. Repairs around the house have become family affairs, with all the older children eager to help. Timmy has infinite patience and love for them, and they respond by pleading to be his helpers. All those helpers slow the job down considerably, but Timmy never seems to notice that. He's having too much fun enjoying his children.

*Comment: Not everyone who lives in the lower frequencies has a happy ending to their story. Timmy's happiness came from finding a person who could love him for his gentleness, and provide him with the structure he needed to continue being productive. Mary was smart enough to realize what a wonderful husband and father Timmy could make, and was more than willing to make up for Timmy's beta deficiencies in exchange for such happiness.*

## *"Last Minute Panic" Peter*

Peter was eleven years old when I met him, and was having trouble with reading comprehension and math. Peter tested at above average intelligence, but did very poorly on quizzes in the classroom.

Peter was a quiet child who inadvertently perturbed teachers by his lack of eye contact when being spoken to. Last year was especially difficult for him because he had a teacher who insisted that legs were to be kept under one's own desk. Peter's legs betrayed him constantly, sneaking out into the aisles while he was off daydreaming in another world. To make things worse, he often did not hear the teacher's first request to get his feet back under the desk.

When I first saw Peter's brain wave pattern, I thought for sure that he was another Trancing Timmy. I was immediately aware of a beautiful symmetry between his hemispheres. His very open theta pattern told me that he had not lost the mystical qualities of early childhood. His very balanced alpha represented a meditative mind and a very active visual imagination. Beta was also well represented in both hemispheres. I was looking at a perfectly lovely, fully functioning range of brain frequencies.

I was also impressed by the innocent openness of his mind. Most adults and young academic achievers usually diminish their lower brain wave activity when first hooked up to the EEG equipment, a natural defense in an assessment situation. Peter showed no self-consciousness even though he fully understood the equipment's capacity. Instead he showed an open curiosity, qualities that are an advantage to learning. I would have been really stumped if I had stopped our session at that point. However, I asked him to read for me.

Peter's brain pattern made an immediate shift to a very imbalanced state. His left hemisphere, which houses his language expression abilities, went into a high magnitude beta panic. This hemispheric imbalance was worsened by a shutdown of the beta in the right hemisphere, the hemisphere he needs to help him comprehend what he reads. The lower frequencies disappeared entirely (within the calibrated range of my biofeedback equipment). Peter's mind was programmed to panic, freeze, and shut down when asked to read.

Peter was so stressed in academic performance situations that he failed by trying too hard. If he could just relax back into his natural pattern, learning would be so much easier for him.

*Comment: Performance anxiety is probably the most common cause of failure to demonstrate what we know. Many people know and understand much more than they can express, making them appear and feel less intelligent than they are. Everyone is naturally motivated to be the best they can be. In fact, it is caring too much that causes the beta panic and shutdown of the lower frequencies. We lose what is most special about ourselves when we care too much about what others think of us.*

## *"Weak Link William"*

William likes school, but he has a lot of trouble concentrating during class time. If you ask him what he likes the best about school, he'll tell you it's seeing his school friends, playground time, lunch, and riding the school bus with his neighborhood friends. He likes to have a good time, and fun is his middle name. Anything active is just his cup of tea. If nothing interesting is happening in the classroom, his impish eyes will dart around the room until he finds another pair of roving eyes, also looking for a little amusement on the side. His teacher calls this "looking for trouble."

William doesn't mean to be a difficult child. He likes his teacher, and doesn't understand why she gets so frustrated with him. William doesn't do well in any academic subject that requires him to sit still for more than a few minutes. He just can't keep his attention on the blackboard or his book long enough to learn.

At home, William's parents also have concerns about his behavior. His non-stop play leaves toys from one end of the house to the other, and he can't seem to remember to pick up after himself. He also doesn't remember to play more quietly when other family members ask for some quiet time. This has made William appear to be insensitive to other people's needs. William seems to mean well, but most everything he is asked to do goes in one ear and out the other.

William's mother has found that the most severe punishment she can give him is to make him sit still for ten minutes with no toys or outside stimulation. William's sparkling personality wilts dramatically when he is not allowed to keep himself busy. His mother says he looks like a man condemned to death at these times. Life seems to drain right out of him. William is diagnosed as having Attention Deficit Disorder with Hyperactivity.

*Comment: What can be done with a child who truly wants to please adults and do well in school, but can't concentrate or hold a thought long enough to do either? Have that child tested for Attention Deficit Disorder.[1] Children do not have to be hyperactive like William to have A.D.D.; however, hyperactivity is common with this disorder.*

*Children with A.D.D. usually are found to have weak electrical firings at the neurochemical sites that allow the various parts of the brain to communicate with each other. Physical hyperactivity may be an attempt to "manually" stimulate their brain as a compensation for its lower voltage.*

---

[1] For more information on Attention Deficit Disorder, read Goldstein and Goldstein, Managing Attention Disorders in Children, New York: John Wiley & Sons, 1990; Wender, Paul, The Hyperactive Child, Adolescent, and Adults: Attention Deficit Disorder Through the Lifespan, New York: Oxford University Press, 1987; and Kelly, Kate, You Mean I'm Not Lazy, Stupid, or Crazy, New York: McMillan, 1995.

*Low brain wave activity in such an active child explains why the drug Ritalin has been helpful to some (not all) children like William. Ritalin is a special neuro-chemical stimulant for the brain. Many people have wondered why a stimulant is able to help a child who already appears overly stimulated. Seeing William's brain wave pattern makes the reason clear. With A.D.D., children's active behavior covers up the real problem — their brain is actually understimulated.*

*Parents who don't like the idea of giving their child a drug, even under the advice of a doctor, may wish to read up on alternative approaches to correcting this organic problem. Some health food stores sell books on nutrition therapy. I don't have enough knowledge on whether these alternative approaches work on true A.D.D. children to make a recommendation one way or the other. (Sometimes food allergies will mimic A.D.D. or ADHD symptoms.) Every parent who decides to treat their child's A.D.D. with Ritalin or another drug must weigh the academic and social benefits derived from using a drug against the possibility of side effects that are present with all prescription drugs. An unbiased doctor can provide you with the information you need to make an educated decision.*

*Adults tend not to compensate for A.D.D. by being hyperactive (ADHD) as much as children do. If you suspect your brain has never been as neurologically active as it should be, or you have experienced chronic poor memory or poor attention span since childhood, then ask yourself the following questions. Can your nutrition be better than it is? Do you get enough sleep and exercise on a daily basis? Are there emotional concerns in your life that are preoccupying your mind? If you are sure none of these factors is causing your poor memory or attention deficit, then consider talking to your doctor.*

*Your brain may be needing a chemical that can be easily supplemented under a doctor's guidance. Sometimes Ritalin can also be effective for adults, and only needs to be taken when cognitive performance is required.*

## *"Chaos Charlie"*

Charlie was an unmanageable child at school. He wouldn't sit still for a minute, and refused to raise his hand in class before asking questions. He was loud and disruptive, and refused to accept any disciplinary action. He knew teachers had no power to physically control him, and he'd use that information to provoke them all the more.

No one knew what Charlie's learning potential was, because he refused to take anything seriously. Some teachers thought he had an attention deficit disorder, others labeled him hyperactive; a few thought he was just a bad kid.

By fourth grade no public school would accept him, and his mother was forced to place him in a special school for mentally disadvantaged children. On the school's request, she brought him to see a psychologist. Charlie refused to shake the man's hand, walked by him into the office, and immediately started going through all the drawers and file cabinets in the room.

The psychologist waited to see how Charlie's mother would handle this, but she did nothing. Charlie pushed everything off the psychologist's desk onto the floor, and still she did nothing. Charlie found a box of tissues and pulled one out after another, throwing them around the room, and she continued to ignore him.

Then Charlie tried throwing a chair against the wall. That got her attention, but she managed to compose herself almost immediately. Turning back to the psychologist, she apologetically said in a sweet, little girl voice, "This is what he is like." The interview wasn't going much better. Every time his mother would talk about Charlie, he would put his hands over his ears, and scream at the top of his lungs.

Then, just as Charlie threatened to rip a page out of a book, the psychologist took over, and removed Charlie from the room. Charlie was handed over to a specialist in behavioral problems while the psychologist took Charlie's history with the mother.

Charlie's father was a here-today, gone-tomorrow friend to the boy. He had not lived with Charlie and his wife in over six years, but he'd walk into their home anytime he wished, acting like he had never been gone. When he was around, he treated Charlie special, taking him fishing and camping.

While his father was back at home, Charlie didn't have to follow any of the rules his mother feebly tried to enforce. His dad treated Charlie's mom disrespectfully, and Charlie learned to do the same. Charlie loved his dad, and was furious with his mom. He blamed her for not being able to keep his father home.

Charlie's behavior problem was obvious. So was its cause. What was left unanswered was whether there might also be learning disabilities, attention deficit disorder or hyperactivity unrelated to Charlie's anger.

His was medically tested for signs of any weak neuro-chemical links. Not only were none found, but Charlie showed ample magnitude in the beta, alpha, and theta frequencies, across both hemispheres. His brain was certainly alive and well, fueled by deep feelings (theta), a good imagination (alpha), and an excellent ability to manipulate adults (beta).

Charlie's wonderful active brain will not be available to him in a productive way until he works through his anger and has consistency in his daily life. His mother is working on this, with the help of a number of professionals.

*Comment: This is a very extreme example of how emotional pain can interfere with learning. Charlie is unhappy and he is angry about it, angry enough to refuse to do anything adults value, until they help him emotionally.*

*Many people can't function without some happiness in their lives. They are the opposite of Anxious Ann, who can put her emotions on the back burner for years and use her beta abilities to gain a sense of control over her life.*

*People like Charlie don't care about doing well in society's eyes unless they are happy. They need to be happy before they can also be successful in life.*

*Additional Comment: In very rare situations destructive or violent behavior can be triggered by a severe chemical or hormonal imbalance or a serious medical illness such as a brain tumor. If you have any doubts, always check with a physician.*

## "Blocked Theta Terry"

Terry knew something was very wrong with her life, but she just couldn't get a handle on what it was. By others' standards, she would have been considered fortunate. She was intelligent enough to have a good job, and pretty enough to always have a boyfriend. Terry had just bought an expensive sporty car she could finally afford, and had one of the most stylish wardrobes of all her friends. But still, she felt empty inside. It didn't make any sense to her, because her life was just as good as people she knew who seemed happy.

Terry decided to enter therapy when her emptiness turned to despair and then to depression. She couldn't motivate herself to go to work anymore, and she was already bored with her newest boyfriend. She spent her first session in therapy crying without understanding why.

Over the weeks Terry recognized the root of her emptiness. Terry had been close to her family when she was young, but turned away from them in her teen years. As soon as she was old enough, she moved out of her parents' home and claimed herself independent.

She didn't need anyone, or so she thought. She tried to make her boyfriends her new family, but they never quite lived up to her expectations. After a while she was agreeing with her girlfriends that there just aren't any good men out there. Terry's world had become empty because she could feel no love in it.

One of Terry's therapy assignments was to list all her memories of times when she had felt happy and "full." Terry list consisted of memories of her parents smiling at her, special holidays with lots of laughter, playing with her little dog when she was young, her grandparents giving her big hugs and reading to her when she was little, nature hikes with her girl scout troop, etc. Every memory on Terry's list was of feeling close to someone or something that was alive: people, animals, and nature.

Terry came to realize that she had closed her heart to love when she left home, determined to not need anyone. This is a mistake that many teenagers make. Terry found out that being independent didn't have to condemn her to being detached from all emotional ties. Terry learned that being a mature adult means that she can be independent in her thoughts and life style while still being emotionally bonded to people who love her.

Understanding that she could let the people who love her back into her life helped Terry to not put such high expectations on the men she dated. One man no longer had to fill all her emotional needs. Terry also started feeling love more deeply. The more she felt love emanating from herself, the less she wanted to pass judgment on her dates and on her family.

Terry feels like her old self again. She's in love with life, just like she remembers when she was young. She's sharing her life with her family again, and looks forward to the day she can share her love with a husband and children.

*Comment: Blocked theta is probably the most overlooked block to learning of all six categories. Unlike Chaos Charlie, who was aware enough of the problem to be angry, most people with blocked theta are numb and empty inside. If they feel anything at all they call it depression, not knowing that they are experiencing the emptiness of a loveless life.*

*Many people make the mistake of pushing themselves through uninteresting jobs or college studies without giving themselves the balance of joyous theta experiences. Without a natural spontaneous openness to love, all of life eventually becomes dull and two-dimensional. Nothing remains interesting enough to learn about.*

## SUMMARY OF CHAPTER 7

| Learning Restrictions: | Common Brain Wave Pattern: |
|---|---|
| Anxiety | high beta, low alpha and theta |
| Trance | high alpha/theta, low beta |
| Last Minute Panic | alternates between anxiety and trance |
| Weak Links | lower brain activity |
| Chaos | all brain wave frequencies active, but unproductive |
| Blocked Theta | all brain wave frequencies active except theta |

Take some time here, before reading on, to assess where you might be on this chart. You probably don't fit any one category all the time. Think instead of when you seem to have the most difficulty learning new information. Which category do you fit most at these times?

| Perceptions Limited to: | Solution: |
|---|---|
| | *Infinity Walk Program in Part III, plus the following:* |
| 2-D | counseling, if needed, to help develop self-esteem separate from work or school performance; needs sensory experiences |
| 3-D and/or Oneness | organizational skills<br>needs a valued 2-D purpose/goal |
| 2-D *or* 3-D and/or Oneness | same as above, plus relaxation techniques, or biofeedback |
| weak or unpredictable | assess nutrition, sleep, exercise; consider medical intervention |
| all may be available, but not focused positively | psychotherapy, medical workup |
| 2-D and 3-D | explore intimacy needs, heal past relationships, connect with nature, explore spirituality |

The Infinity Walk Sensorimotor Program in Part III of this book can help with all these categories, but some of them also deserve the special attention suggested in this chapter.

# CHAPTER 8

# Understanding Your Brain's Current Sensorimotor Pattern

## EYE, EAR, AND HAND DOMINANCE

Brain wave frequencies are one factor to consider when trying to understand how your brain can block new learnings. A second equally important factor is your sensorimotor pattern (of your sensory and motor nervous system). Just as you have a favorite hand for certain skills like writing and holding a fork, you also have a favorite eye and ear. Together, your favorite (or dominant) eye, ear and hand create a sensorimotor network for perceiving, learning, and performing in the world. How cooperative this neural network is, depends on how well integrated your sensory and motor nervous system is.

A short review of the sensory and motor functions of the nervous system will help in understanding the importance of considering neurological dominance patterns in understanding learning blocks.

Our nervous system has two primary functions, sensory and motor. The sensory system takes in information about our environment as well as about our own body, through our sensing organs. These include seeing, hearing, touching, smelling, tasting and sensing movement, pressure, temperature, equilibrium, and sensing where someone or something is located in relationship to ourselves (spatial ability). The motor system operates through our muscles, and is responsible for all actions, including many internal functions and speech.

89

Ideally, all of our senses work together to provide us with the best possible sensory information available in any given situation. I stress the word "ideally" here. Our brains carefully consider our senses' combined awareness of a given situation. They also quickly check our past memories for similar situations, looking for additional insight. Ideally, these immediate sensory impressions will be cross-checked with the sensory memories that have accumulated through our past experiences.

Then some important internal questions will be asked. Have I seen, heard, felt, tasted, or smelled this before? If so, when, and in what circumstances? Do those circumstances apply to this situation? Are any of my senses being negatively biased by a specific past memory? Would it be wise to act differently than one or all of my senses are suggesting, because of some misinterpreted past experience? This internal process goes on in seconds, often outside of our consciousness. We can call this process wisdom, intuition, or just plain common sense.

If an action response is needed, the decision is handed over to the motor system, which is actually just a worker waiting for instructions from the administrative brain. Ideally, this action system, composed mainly of muscles, has a close enough relationship to the rest of our brain to be able to understand its orders exactly as they are intended. Again, this is ideally. If it fails to understand its directions then it will do a poor job of representing our wishes.

As you can see, there are many places this system can break down. Some of the senses may fail to cooperate with other senses, causing confusion. Most of our senses have two sense organs, such as two eyes, ears, and hands. Things can become very confused when they report different information, as sometimes happens. Sometimes two of the senses start fighting for importance, and if one wins, the other will stop reporting effectively. Other times, one of the senses withdraws from active involvement with our environment because it was emotionally hurt by what it saw, or heard, or felt. When this happens the other senses try their best to cover for the weakened sensory input; but good intentions can't prevent absent information from biasing the brain's interpretation of a situation.

Optimally, we need to have all our senses cooperating before we can make wise decisions. This doesn't mean we can't get by just fine without a sense organ operating. Many people do. However, if we are not known to have a sensory organ handicap (such as lack of sight or hearing), then schools, jobs, and society expect us to operate as if all our senses are functioning optimally. If they're not, then we end up feeling like a failure. The truth is, very few people have optimal sensory functioning.

What about the motor system? Let's assume we do not have any permanent physical handicaps. Can our motor systems fail us? Not intentionally, but if they are prevented from receiving important information from our senses and sensory memory, they won't know how to behave appropriately. Our motor system may inadvertently make us look clumsy or say something thoughtless or seemingly unintelligent.

We can only appear to be wise or intelligent if our motor systems are able to represent our intentions. We may have brilliant ideas waiting to be shared with the world, but if the relationship of our senses and sensory memory to our motor system isn't a close one, we'll never be able to demonstrate our abilities.

Our motor nervous system, because it is largely composed of muscle, needs to be kept in good physical shape. We sometimes forget that the health of our brains depends on the health of our bodies (and vice versa). The ability of our muscles to carry out our intentions depends on the coordination of our bodies. Unfortunately, our highly technological world is constantly coming up with new ways to help us avoid using our bodies. Today, many of us have to make a special effort just to keep our bodies exercised.

Sensorimotor cooperation cannot be strengthened and fine tuned without involving the appropriate muscles. However, just practicing something incorrectly over and over again is a very primitive and ineffective use of this principle. The Infinity Walk Sensorimotor Program in Part III of this book has been specially developed to overcome these problems.

## ASSESSING OUR SENSORIMOTOR PATTERN

Before moving on to the Infinity Walk Program it can be very insightful to understand how your present neurological pattern may have been limiting and benefiting you. So, let's first take a few minutes to determine your present sensory pattern for vision and hearing, and your motor pattern as demonstrated through your hands. The more you understand how your neurological pattern has affected your perceptions, your decision-making process, and your successes and failures, the more you will be able to use them as an asset instead of a handicap. Neurological patterns originate from our genetics and life circumstances, but we do not have to be limited to them if we know how to expand our sensorimotor capacity.

Our dominant eye, ear, and hand show natural leadership. Their confidence in taking charge is based on better neural networking and communication with our brains than their non-dominant partner has had the opportunity to develop.

Which eye, ear, and hand are favored in different circumstances can reveal a lot about your special qualities, as well as your less developed potentials. This next section will show you how to determine your eye, ear, and hand dominance. Then, I'll help you interpret what your particular neurological pattern means.

## *Determining Eye Dominance*

The following is a simple accurate method for determining eye dominance. Cut a small hole (no larger than one inch wide) in the center of a plain sheet of writing or typing paper. Ask the person you are assessing to hold the paper with *both hands* and look at your nose through the hole. Write down which of their two eyes you can see more of through the hole. Remember, since they are facing you, their right eye is on your left side, and vice versa. Be especially careful to record the response correctly.

*A Test For Eye Dominance*

To test your own eye dominance (and provide a second test for others) place a penny on the floor. Use *both hands again* to hold the paper about 12-18 inches away from your face; then look through the hole at the penny on the floor. Once you find the penny, *do not move the paper or your head*. Holding still, close one eye. Notice which eye you decided to close first. With this eye closed, can you still see the penny? Next, *again without moving the paper or your head,* open the eye that is closed, and close your other eye. Can you see the penny now? For most people closing one of their eyes will cause the penny to disappear.

Here is the explanation behind eye dominance. The dominant eye feels such a responsibility to absorb all visual information that it will hold on to the image of the penny whether or not the non-dominant eye is allowed to help. When there is only room for one eye to look through the hole in the paper, the dominant eye will be the one to do it. The more the dominant eye likes to be in charge, the more of that eye will be seen through the hole from the other side. When the dominance is extreme it might be more susceptible to eye strain than the other eye. Sometimes, dominance is so obvious you can guess it by just looking at someone's face. The dominant eye may protrude more, or have more wrinkles around it, or seem to have more sparkle or depth than the other eye. Also, some people have a habit of tilting their heads a little to put their dominant eye higher, or more forward than their non-dominant eye.

A third but less accurate test is to ask the person to wink. This test has commonly been used in the past to quickly determine eye dominance. The assumption is that the dominant eye will be kept open. However, I have not found this to always be the case. This may be because the muscles around the dominant eye on some people are more responsive and refined, making it more natural for the brain to communicate with them. Thus, some people may wink with the dominant eye, while others can't even close their dominant eye unless both eyes close together.

Some people switch dominance, depending on the task. I've seen children tilt their heads so their left eye is higher for drawing, and then tilt it to the opposite side so their right eye is higher when they want to access their language communication center to print their name under the drawing. For young children who are still integrating their brain hemispheres this is a perfectly fine compensation. However, for the older student or adult, it shows a lack of hemispheric cooperation for vision, and can eventually cause muscular tension. Accomplishments always come easier when the full brain is cooperating. Eye strain in one eye more than the other, headaches, tiredness, and stiff neck and shoulders can all be indications that your eyes are not cooperating with each other as well as they could.

If you haven't determined your own eye dominance yet, do so now, before we go on. Record all your findings, including any comments. A *Summary Page* has been provided on page 97 of this chapter to use as a guide.

## *Determining Ear Dominance*

A simple test for ear dominance can be done by observing your telephone behavior.[1] Many people will favor one ear for listening on the phone. Sometimes the position of

---

[1] A much more elaborate system for determining ear dominance was created by Thomas Blakeslee. Called a dichotic listening test, the ears are fed different sounds and words simultaneously through stereo earphones. Assuming hearing is good in both ears, the ear that recognized the most sounds and words is considered to be dominant. Blakeslee, Thomas R. *The Right Brain: A New Understanding of the Unconscious Mind and Its Creative Powers.* Garden City, NY: Prentice-Hall, 1977. Cited in Cherry, C., Godwin, D., and Staples, J., *Is the Left Brain Always Right?* Belmont, CA: Fearon Teacher Aids, 1989.

the phone on a desk, or needing to write a message while on the phone, will cause you to use your less dominant ear. So, observe your behavior over a number of circum-stances. When having a casual phone conversation with equally easy left or right access to the phone, which ear do you prefer? If your ear dominance is very strong, you'll only switch to your less dominant ear when the dominant one gets tired.

An extremely strong right ear dominant person may choose to hold the phone to their dominant right ear with a raised shoulder while writing a message with their right hand, rather than give up control to their less dominant left ear for even a minute. If one ear is significantly more dominant than the other, conversations over the phone may sound very different from one ear to the other. The non-dominant ear may seem to be listening to a long-distance conversation, or you may not feel as in touch with the person you are speaking with.

This telephone observation is not meant to measure the ability to hear, which only a doctor or ear specialist can determine. What we are looking for is a subtle sense of preference for listening with one ear over the other. Just as the paper with the hole in it forces us to use our preferred eye, the telephone forces us to use our preferred ear.

When assessing others, try to set up your test conditions so they do not bias the results. For instance, the location of the phone should create easy access for both left and right ear listening. A cordless portable phone or a wall hung phone with the cord hanging below create no bias for left or right-handed people. Locate your test phone where someone can sit and relax and have an extended casual conversation. Don't tell people ahead of time what you are looking for, so they don't unconsciously give you what they think you are looking for.

Once you are satisfied with the information you have gained through observation, you can ask the people you are observing about their telephone behavior without biasing the results. Are they aware of having a preferred ear? Do they use a different ear for different types of phone conversations? Do they enjoy long conversations on the phone, or do they feel at a disadvantage on the phone?

This last question can help determine how dominant their hearing is over other senses, such as vision or touch. People with strong auditory dominance can feel very comfortable having an intimate conversation on the phone. Their capacity to pick up every subtlety in the voice reduces their need to have the person physically present in order to feel connected. People who have a very strong visual or kinesthetic sense, or who have a very undeveloped auditory sense, can feel at a terrible disadvantage when trying to express their feelings over the phone. This frustration often leads to rather short conversations.

Record your observations as well as the person's comments and insights. Note which ear is preferred, and whether the telephone might be a very comfortable or uncomfortable mode of communicating feelings for them. Be sure to determine your own ear dominance as well. Save this information for later use.

## *Determining Hand Dominance*

Our hands give us sensory information through their nerve endings; we call this touch or kinesthetic awareness. They also perform motor movements through their muscles. Therefore, hands have both a sensory and motor function we'll need to be aware of. These two separate functions can sometimes confuse people when they try to decide on which hand is dominant. Usually, the hand we write and hold a fork with is considered to be our dominant hand. Even this can become unclear after hearing stories of children being forced to become right-handed early in life. Then, there are all the people who claim to be ambidextrous. We can quickly make sense out of all of this if we follow the same thought process we have been using in determining eye and ear dominance.

If our hand dominance is extreme we will always use the same hand to do an activity, even to a point of discomfort or lost efficiency. In washing down the walls of your shower stall, or in painting a wall, are you limited to using only one hand? Can you switch the sponge or paint brush from hand to hand, or are you forced to continually position your body in order to reach with only one arm? If so, you may be behaving as if your non-dominant hand is handicapped. This can account for significant differences in muscle strength between your two arms. Muscles must be used to be developed.

### AMBIDEXTERITY AND MIXED DOMINANCE

True ambidexterity is the ability to use both hands with equal ease on the same task. If you can throw a ball, hammer a nail, or thread a needle with equal ease regardless of which hand you use, then you are ambidextrous for these tasks. This is different from someone who writes with their right hand, but throws a ball with their left, which is dominance switching — just like children who switch from right to left eye dominance by tilting their heads when moving from printing to drawing a picture. This switching shows a high degree of creative compensation, but it is not the same thing as operating from full neurological integration.

Without the rare early childhood benefit of being reinforced for approaching all tasks from an ambidextrous awareness, our motor response to sensory input will vary from one side of our body to another. Concert pianists can tell you about their long hours of training to make their hands equally responsive to the piano keys.

To determine whether you have some ambidextrous or switching abilities, make a list of the tasks you can do equally well with both hands, and which you consistently do well with only your left or right hand.

What about people who think they should have been left-handed, but remember being encouraged to switch, by a parent or teacher, when they were young? Sometimes, this may be exactly what happened; some adult assumed right handedness was a favored way to be in the world, without taking into account the child's eye dominance. A matching eye-hand dominance can be helpful in writing, throwing a ball, and other eye-hand coordination tasks. Having your dominant eye and hand operate through the same brain hemisphere gives them a greater ease in commu-nicating and cooperating with one another. If you are one of these people who intu-itively feel you should have been left-handed, you may find that either your dominant eye or ear is on the left side.

Make a note as to whether your hand dominance is on the same side as your eye and ear dominance. If all three are not, then you have a mixed dominance. If your hand dominance is different from your eye and ear dominance, you may find that it is sometimes difficult to express yourself through your body in general, or through writing in particular.

If your eye and ear dominance are on opposite sides, things can get very interesting. Each hand may choose to follow the sensory organ that is dominant on its side of the body. Using piano playing as an example, a dominant right eye may encourage good sight reading of the music and easily relay this visual information to the right hand, because of the right eye's close connection to the language communication center in the brain. Simultaneously, the dominant left ear may encourage the left hand to play "by ear." The hands may constantly get confused until the pianist's training is advanced enough to both sight-read and play by ear simultaneously. Until then, the struggle between the two sides will alternately cause missed notes and lost rhythm.

## *Summary of Your Sensorimotor Pattern*

Circle below your dominant eye, ear, and hand. If you sometimes switch dominance, circle both the left and right, but make a heavier line around the one you use most.

Eye Dominance:                Left Eye                        Right Eye
(circle one)                                               (language advantage)

Comments:

Ear Dominance:                Left Ear                        Right Ear
(circle one)                                               (language advantage)

Comments:

Hand Dominance:               Left Hand                       Right Hand
(circle one)                                               (language advantage)

Comments:

Next, put an extra heavy circle around your response for eye or ear dominance, if you believe you rely on one sense more than the other (e.g., you are more of a visual or auditory learner).

Now you can summarize your pattern here. Select one of the possible eight neurological patterns. If you believe you are predominantly visual or auditory, circle the stronger sense as well.

All Dominance on the Same Side of the Body

1.   Right Eye, Right Ear, Right Hand
2.   Left Eye, Left Ear, Left Hand

Dominant Eye on Opposite Side from Dominant Ear and Hand

3.   Right Eye, Left Ear, Left Hand
4.   Left Eye, Right Ear, Right Hand

Dominant Ear on Opposite Side from Dominant Eye and Hand

5.   Right Eye, Left Ear, Right Hand
6.   Left Eye, Right Ear, Left Hand

Dominant Hand on Opposite Side from Dominant Eye and Ear

7.   Right Eye, Right Ear, Left Hand
8.   Left Eye, Left Ear, Right Hand

# UNDERSTANDING YOUR SENSORIMOTOR DOMINANCE PATTERN

To learn more about yourself, find your dominance pattern on the following pages. All eight patterns assume the normal left hemisphere placement of the language communication center, giving the right dominant eye, ear, and hand the language communication advantage. (This will be true for 95% of the population.) Our nerves and muscles are operated by the brain hemisphere on the opposite side. Hence, the "wires" cross over from left to right, or right to left.

### 1.   Right Eye, Right Ear, Right Hand

*Advantages:*

This pattern is least likely to have academic problems in school, since it has the greatest access to the language communication center in the left hemisphere. Having all dominances on the same side helps them work together more efficiently, making successes more likely. This pattern is most valued by our society because of our high regard for language skills. Highly successful people with this pattern have the capacity to focus on their goals; they are action people who make things happen in their business and community. These advantages are reduced if the lower brain wave functions are not allowed any importance.

*Disadvantages:*

When academic and learning problems do occur, they tend to reflect too much focus on language-related beta details; not seeing the forest for the trees. If reading is difficult, it is usually because they are over focusing on each letter or each word; they fail by trying too hard. These people could benefit from less structure, less concern over rules, and more spontaneous action. If they have overly relied on the right side of their body, they may feel uncoordinated in their gross motor (full body) movements. If their easy access to their language communication center has caused them to overly rely on the beta realm, they may tend toward nervousness, perfectionism, and fear of failure. Poor memory can result from trying to consciously hold on to countless details, not trusting they can be retrieved later out of the depths of the mysterious gray matter of the right hemisphere. If someone with this pattern experiences a great deal of academic difficulty, their access to the right (opposite) hemisphere may be found to be inadequate. In extreme cases, the use of Ritalin has been helpful.

Take a few minutes to write down your thoughts and insights.

## 2. Left Eye, Left Ear, Left Hand

*Advantages:*

Although some initial language advantage may be lost in this pattern due to a weaker connection with the language center located in the left hemisphere, having all dominance on the same side is still a big advantage in academic education.[2] Visual and auditory learning is in harmony with paper and pencil demonstrations of knowledge. With sufficient motivation and support, people with this pattern can develop good, consistent access to their language center early in life, and still maintain a unique pre-language, sensory perspective on beta knowledge. At their best, these people can display a magical command over language and symbols, and constantly amaze you with their innovative thinking. These talents may be more appreciated in artistic or philosophical communities.

---

[2] Read *The Throwing Madonna,* by William Calvin for an excellent review of how humans' evolutionary process may determine the development of the language center in the left hemisphere rather than the right (New York: McGraw-Hill, 1983).

*Disadvantages:*

Along with some of the best advantages, this pattern can also cause challenging disadvantages. Too much focus on language generated beta values early in life can cause this child to go to one of three extremes. (1) Early frustration can cause the child to abandon interest in developing a stronger connection with the language center. (2) Early importance placed on language and academic success may cause stressful beta over-achievement and the devaluing of their natural connection to the sensory realm. (3) They may find themselves switching between the two realms, confusing themselves and others with the inconsistency in their behaviors and abilities.

*Note: Relatively few people have this neurological combination. Some of them may have their language center located in the right hemisphere, giving them the same advantages of the Right-Right-Right dominance pattern with left hemisphere placement of the language center.*

Take a few minutes to write down your thoughts and insights.

### 3. Right Eye, Left Ear, Left Hand

*Advantages:*

The close ear-hand relationship could make it easier to demonstrate knowledge received through hearing, but only if this is also the dominant sense. If these people are not held back by learning handicaps, they could develop natural abilities for creative expression in writing, music, storytelling, acting, etc. Musical ability might be related to "playing by ear"; sight-reading music may be more difficult. Demonstration of creative abilities may not have surfaced yet if these people tend toward a stronger visual than auditory dominance, because of the lack of motor support for visual tasks.

*Advantages of opposite eye-ear dominance:*

This pattern represents a mixed sensory dominance, making it more likely that this person will switch back and forth between a visual and auditory preference, depending on the task. In either case, one or both of the senses are usually overly developed to make up for the lack of support of the remaining sense. This can create stress, but it can also facilitate unusual talent relating to one of the senses.

*Disadvantages of opposite eye-ear dominance:*

Early confusion between when to allow the visual versus the auditory sense to take charge of learning can cause academic frustration and sense of failure. Switching between the two senses can also become tension producing, causing tiredness or headaches. Until seeing and hearing begin to operate together, a person with this combination may not look and listen at the same time. If visual preference is chosen, the person may be criticized for looking right at another person but not hearing what they are saying. If auditory preference is chosen, the person may be criticized for not looking at someone when being spoken to, even though he or she may be listening. This switching also gives some people a feeling of having two different personalities, depending on what they are focusing on. Hence, some will have uncomfortable discrepancies in career and lifestyle interests (e.g., I'd like to either teach business law at Harvard, or be a forest ranger at a reclusive outpost in Montana).

*Disadvantages of opposite eye-hand dominance:*

This combination can produce poor eye-hand coordination. There may be difficulties with playing ball, handwriting, drawing, fine motor tasks, and sight-reading music. Since visual memory is not well integrated with the writing hand, errors in writing can be expected. These would include reversals, misspellings, leaving out letters, numbers, and even whole words. Visual reaction time may be slowed, unless the person disciplines him or herself to be vigilant. However, this could result in a visually intense person who is prone to stress.

Take a few minutes to write down your thoughts and insights.

## 4. Left Eye, Right Ear, Right Hand

*Advantages:*

The strong relationship between the right ear and hand, and the language center in the left hemisphere, can help this person excel verbally at a very young age (unless there is a strong visual preference that diverts this person's development of vocal abilities). The early verbal skills help the child join into the world of adults sooner. The person may develop a love of verbal language, including the use of wit and satire. At their best, these people will also have the advantage of seeing things in a somewhat different way. This may spark a creative desire in them, but the actual completion of a creative project may be slowed down by their opposing eye-hand dominance.

*Advantages of opposite eye-ear dominance:*

This pattern represents a mixed sensory dominance, making it more likely that this person will switch back and forth between a visual and auditory preference, depending on the task. In either case, one or both of the senses are usually overly developed to make up for the lack of support of the remaining sense. This can create stress, but it can also facilitate unusual talent relating to one of the senses.

*Disadvantages of an unsupported left eye dominance:*

Learning to read the English language can be difficult for the left eye dominant person. Having to scan a book from left to right, rather than right to left, puts these people at a slight disadvantage. These early reading frustrations may take their toll on a child's self esteem, and can continue to make a negative impact years later, even after the person has learned to read adequately through various neurological compensations.

*Disadvantages of opposite eye-hand dominance:*

This combination can produce poor eye-hand coordination. There may be difficulties with playing ball, handwriting, drawing, fine motor tasks, and sight-reading music. Since visual memory is not well integrated with the writing hand, errors in writing can be expected. These would include reversals, misspellings, leaving out letters, numbers, and even whole words. Visual reaction time may be slowed, unless the person disciplines him or herself to be vigilant. However, this could result in a visually intense person who is prone to stress.

*Disadvantages of opposite eye-ear dominance:*

Early confusion between when to allow the visual versus the auditory senses to take charge of learning can cause academic frustration and sense of failure. Switching between the two senses can also become tension producing, causing tiredness or headaches. Until seeing and hearing begin to operate together, a person with this combination may not look and listen at the same time. If visual preference is chosen, the person may be criticized for looking right at another person but not hearing what they are saying. If auditory preference is chosen, the person may be criticized for not looking at someone when being spoken to, even though he or she may be listening. Switching also gives some people a feeling of having two different personalities, depending on what they are focusing on. Hence, some will have uncomfortable discrepancies in career and lifestyle interests (e.g., I'd like to either teach business law at Harvard, or be a forest ranger at a reclusive outpost in Montana).

Take a few minutes to write down your thoughts and insights.

### 5. Right Eye, Left Ear, Right Hand

*Advantages:*

Eye-hand coordination is maintained in this combination. Academic studies and testing requiring vision, visual memory, and paper and pencil testing are not compromised by this pattern (unless there is a strong auditory preference). As with all mixed patterns, the handicapping of one dominant sense can force the other two to develop stronger abilities as a form of compensation. In this case, if vision is chosen as the more valued sense, excellent visual perception and/or photographic memory can result. Graphic arts and technical writing and attention to detail would be natural abilities. Since hearing stands alone without other support, this combination may cause some early learning frustrations. This would be especially true if the person's learning style is more auditory than visual. However, after they catch up, left ear dominant people can excel at careers needing acute auditory awareness, such as counseling and music.

*Advantages of opposite eye-ear dominance:*

This pattern represents a mixed sensory dominance, making it more likely that this person will switch back and forth between a visual and auditory preference, depending on the task. In either case, one or both of the senses are usually overly developed to make up for the lack of support of the remaining sense. This can create stress, but it can also facilitate unusual talent relating to one of the senses.

*Disadvantages of opposite eye-ear dominance:*

Early confusion between when to allow the visual versus the auditory senses to take charge of learning can cause academic frustration and sense of failure. Switching between the two senses can also become tension producing, causing tiredness or headaches. Until seeing and hearing begin to operate together, a person with this combination may not look and listen at the same time. If visual preference is chosen, the person may be criticized for looking right at another person but not hearing what they are saying. If auditory preference is chosen, the person may be criticized for not looking at someone when being spoken to, even though he or she may be listening. Switching also gives some people a feeling of having two different personalities, depending on what they are focusing on. Hence, some will have uncomfortable discrepancies in career and lifestyle interests (e.g., I'd like to either teach business law at Harvard, or be a forest ranger at a reclusive outpost in Montana).

*Disadvantages of opposite ear-hand dominance:*

Poor neurological networking, between auditory input and writing, can cause simple errors, making a person appear less intelligent. The person with this pattern can't always trust that their hand will write what their dominant ear is hearing. Reversals of numbers, such as phone numbers, are common, when dictated. This can be corrected by seeing each number mentally before writing it down. Early spelling difficulties arise when spelling is taught phonetically. This person should be encouraged to learn spelling through the development of visual memory. The section in chapter 11 on verbal/linguistic intelligence explains how to do this. Reaction time to auditory input may be slower. Since speech is produced through motor movements, this person may need more time to formulate their responses to conversation. They may speak slowly, and sometimes need to search for just the right words to express themselves. Even those who show no verbal handicap as an adult may mention having been a quiet listener as a child.

Take a few minutes to write down your thoughts and insights.

## 6.  Left Eye, Right Ear, Left Hand

*Advantages:*

Eye-hand coordination is maintained in this combination. Academic studies and testing requiring vision, visual memory, and paper and pencil testing gain some advantage by this pattern. (The eye-hand advantage could be greatly reduced if there is a strong auditory preference.) However, since the dominant left eye and hand are not in close relationship with the language communication center in the brain, there may be a somewhat slower start to learning in the early school years. As with all mixed patterns, the handicapping of one dominant sense can force the other two to develop stronger abilities as a form of compensation. In this case, if vision is chosen as the more valued sense, visual creativity may develop. Since hearing stands alone without other support, this combination may cause some early learning frustrations. However, after they catch up, these people can excel at verbal skills as well.

*Advantages of opposite eye-ear dominance:*

This pattern represents a mixed sensory dominance, making it more likely that this person will switch back and forth between a visual and auditory preference, depending on the task. In either case, one or both of the senses are usually overly developed to make up for the lack of support of the remaining sense. This can create stress, but it can also facilitate unusual talent relating to one of the senses.

*Disadvantages of opposite eye-ear dominance:*

Early confusion between when to allow the visual versus the auditory senses to take charge of learning can cause academic frustration and sense of failure. Switching between the two senses can also become tension producing, causing tiredness or headaches. Until seeing and hearing begin to operate together, a person with this combination may not look and listen at the same time. If visual preference is chosen, the person may be criticized for looking right at another person but not hearing what they are saying. If auditory preference is chosen, the person may be criticized for not looking at someone when being spoken to, even though he or she may be listening. Switching also gives some people a feeling of having two different personalities, depending on what they are focusing on. Hence, some will have uncomfortable discrepancies in career and lifestyle interests (e.g., I'd like to either teach business law at Harvard, or be a forest ranger at a reclusive outpost in Montana).

*Disadvantages of opposite ear-hand dominance:*

Poor neurological networking, between auditory input and writing, can cause simple errors, making a person appear less intelligent. The person with this pattern can't always trust that their hand will write what their dominant ear is hearing. Reversals of numbers, such as phone numbers, are common, when dictated. This can be corrected by seeing each number mentally before writing it down. Early spelling difficulties arise when spelling is taught phonetically. This person should be encouraged to learn spelling through visual memory. The section in chapter 11 on verbal/linguistic intelligence explains how to do this. Reaction time to auditory input may be slower. Since speech is produced through motor movements, this person may need more time to formulate their responses to conversation. They may speak slowly, and sometimes need to search for just the right words to express themselves. Even those who show no verbal handicap as an adult may mention having been a quiet listener as a child.

Take a few minutes to write down your thoughts and insights.

### 7. Right Eye, Right Ear, Left Hand

*Advantages:*

Eye-ear cooperation is fully maintained in this pattern, and directly linked to the language center, *if* it is located in the left hemisphere. Therefore this person's verbal communication skills may be advantaged. The sensory advantages (eye and ear) of this pattern are the same as for the Right-Right-Right pattern reviewed on pages 98-99. If they experience any problems in conversation, it would most likely be caused by the unsupported motor functions of speaking, which can be strengthened by the Infinity Walk Program.

This is a relatively rare pattern. Though this pattern may have been inherited, it is also possible that the sensory *or* motor dominance switched hemispheres before or shortly after birth, due to some form of trauma to the brain.[3] This is nothing to be concerned about. These early adjustments in the brain are a sign of excellent survival ability!

*Disadvantages of dominant hand opposite dominant eye and ear:*

This pattern could create frustration over performance. Since neither the visual nor the auditory senses are closely connected with the motor response system, it could sometimes feel difficult to express your talents, abilities, and knowledge. Some people compensate for this pattern by being methodical about their work. Others develop a less vigilant attitude, and stop trying to be productive. The *Infinity Walk Sensorimotor Program* would be especially valuable to you, since it increases sensory and motor cooperation across hemispheres.

## 8.  Left Eye, Left Ear, Right Hand

*Advantages:*

The sensory advantages (eye and ear) of this pattern are the same as for the Left-Left-Left pattern reviewed on page 99. A unique, pre-language sensory perspective on beta knowledge may be maintained. At their best, these people may display a magical command over language and symbolism, or have very rich sensory lives.

*Disadvantages of dominant hand opposite dominant eye and ear:*

There is some possibility that this person was meant to be left-handed but was switched to right by a well intended adult; or, some form of mild brain trauma occurred before or shortly after birth, causing the sensory control for sight and hearing to re-locate to the right hemisphere. (See #7 *Right-Right-Left*, and footnote 3 for more information.)

This pattern could create frustration over performance. Since neither the visual nor the auditory senses are closely connected with the motor response system, it could sometimes feel difficult to express your talents, abilities, and

---

[3] The following books are good medical and psychiatric sources for understanding hemispheric specialization as a consequence of trauma. Benson D. Frank, and Zaidel, Eran. (Ed.) The Dual Brain: Hemispheric Specialization in Humans. New York: The Guilford Press, 1985. Galaburda, Albert M. (Ed.) Dyslexia and Development: Neurobiological Aspects of Extra-Ordinary Brains. Cambridge MA: Harvard University Press, 1993.

knowledge. Some people compensate for this pattern by being methodical about their work. Others develop a less vigilant attitude, and stop trying to be productive. The Infinity Walk Sensorimotor Program would be especially valuable to you since it increases sensory and motor cooperation across hemispheres.

Take a few minutes to write down your thoughts and insights.


## KNOWING YOUR PATTERN

Why is it so important to know your dominant sensorimotor pattern?

Remember that the motor system is merely carrying out orders based on sensory input and childhood conditioning. How it carries them out can tell us a lot about how our unique sensory network perceives everything in life. Our sensory system has the power of shaping and coloring our personal concept of reality. Should we let it operate unconsciously, or should we learn all we can about it, so we can be in charge of it? By now, you have a pretty good idea of your present sensorimotor strengths, as well as how your neural networking would benefit from further attention and development.

Part III will guide you through the Infinity Walk Sensorimotor Program developed specifically to help you strengthen the sensorimotor pathways that would most benefit you.

CHAPTER 9

# Classroom Clues to Sensorimotor Blocks

**H**ave you ever had this happen to you? You read or hear something that makes complete sense to you at the time, but later you're not able to explain it to someone else, or worse yet, to yourself. How about this one? You studied for an exam and felt confident that you would do well, but when the actual test questions were put in front of you, you couldn't remember the answers, even though you knew them just the night before.

Or this one? You carefully read how to put something together that you just bought from a store. You look over the instructions and review the diagrams and it doesn't look too difficult. Then when you try to actually put the merchandise together, nothing makes sense anymore.

Here are some more:

*You have a favorite song, and know all the words, but you're not able to sing it correctly.*

*You admire a beautiful tree in your yard that you have been looking at for years, but when you try to draw it, your drawing looks nothing like the tree at all.*

*Someone gives you their telephone number but you write it down incorrectly.*

*You've never been able to dance to the rhythm of music.*

*You think that you couldn't learn a musical instrument to save your life.*

*High school sports were a total embarrassment for you.*

*You practice what you want to say to someone, but when you try to say it, it comes out all wrong.*

*You get lost when you try to find a new place using a map.*

*No matter how hard you try, you never seem to get the promotions at work that you believe you deserve.*

*You know you're smart, but you can't seem to convince anyone else that you are.*

These are all examples of situations that require our sensory and motor nervous system to work together. I'll explain exactly what these two interrelated systems of nerves do in a minute. But first, look over the above list again. Were there some things listed that you automatically assumed you shouldn't be able to do, because you don't have a "natural talent" for them? Were there things listed that you would love to be able to do, but think it is out of the realm of possibilities for you? If so, read these next paragraphs carefully; they are especially for you.

We are all whole beings. Unless we have experienced serious neurological damage sometime since the conception of our life, we have the full potential to use all of our brain in daily living. However, for some reason not fully understood, most of us tend to show a preference for using some of our brain capacities over others. This preference creates a habitual neurological pattern that can facilitate some skills and abilities but hinder others.

All of us have neurologically handicapped ourselves in some way. Some of these sensorimotor handicaps go unnoticed during the school years because they are not valued by our formal educational system. For instance, schools don't test us on the ability to walk and carry on an intelligent conversation at the same time, yet many people cannot do this. Other handicaps are noticed in school but given no value. Only the music teacher cared if we were tone deaf, and we would not have failed the course because of it. At worst, we might have been asked to mouth the words instead of attempting to sing. Unfortunately, some sensorimotor blocks are taken so seriously in school that children wear the label of failure inside their heads the rest of their lives.

I know a voice therapist in Toronto, Canada who can take so-called tone deaf adults and transform their monotone sound into a musical scale in one session. In no time at all, she has them singing melodies, on pitch, for the first time in their lives. Why should we expect any less from other forms of sensorimotor blocks?

Getting the sensorimotor system to cooperate, as this voice therapist does, is a lot easier than drilling content. These formerly "tone deaf" students had a long school history of not being able to carry a tune. A hundred songs or more had probably been tried on them throughout the years in school. Obviously, *practice has nothing to do with it; getting the sensorimotor system to cooperate is the solution.*

**In fact, every success and failure that life brings us, all our hidden insecurities over performance, every moment of self doubt before we take on a new challenge, and much of what allows us to feel good about ourselves, is intimately wrapped up in our own particular sensorimotor pattern of habits. Understanding our present sensorimotor pattern can help in breaking through these neurological habits, allowing for spontaneity and excellence in daily life.**

Early sensorimotor blocks to learning can hold back life successes for anyone. I asked American members of MENSA, an international organization for people who have an IQ score in the top 2% of the population, if any of them had experienced early academic problems. I received a number of responses from members who had been thought to be learning disabled.[1]

Today their careers include building contractor, landscaper, electrician, educator, librarian, model ship builder, small business owner, older returning college student, and computer scientist. A number of these high IQ individuals reported struggling with low self-esteem for years after their early academic failures. Some of them did not gain sufficient confidence in their intelligence to attempt college until they entered their 40's. The first half of their lives had been spent compensating for early blocks to learning and living within the resulting limitations.

---

[1] Thank you for the many responses I received from the request I placed in the June 1993 Mensa Bulletin. Some responses also came from students who excelled in academics but were very bored by the school program, and from students who felt isolated from their peers due to their high intelligence. Thank you for these responses as well.

By the time we have out-grown school, most of us have become excellent compensators. As we enter adulthood, we put our energies into what we do best and become successful in one area of life, avoiding others like the plague. Taken to the extreme, this concentration of energy has produced some "one-track" geniuses, to the world's benefit. This book is not necessarily for these rare people, unless in their equally rare moments of not focusing on their life's work, they find themselves unhappy and isolated from the vast richness life has to offer.

Regardless of how each of us has learned to live with the shortcomings of our present neurological pattern, understanding it as a body/kinesthetic habit from early childhood is an important step to increasing choices and opportunities in our lives.[2]

## CLUES IN THE CLASSROOM

Observing students learn Infinity Walk over the last eight years has given me a real opportunity to pinpoint certain behavioral signs that represent less than optimal sensorimotor integration. I've listed these indicators for you, followed by a brief explanation of each of them. Some will seem obvious; I think you'll find others of them thought-provoking. If you recognize yourself or someone you are working with in one or more of these categories, then Infinity Walk can be especially helpful to you.

---

[2] Some, if not all dominance patterns have genetic or organic beginnings. However, the automatic habit for these patterns is strengthened by not stretching ourselves past the comfort zone in learning, thereby restricting ourselves forever.

1. **STUDENT'S PHYSICAL COORDINATION IS BELOW AVERAGE FOR AGE**

Below average coordination may relate to the student's neurological inability to put sensory information into action. Command of the motor nervous system has yet to be developed. Some children are just naturally slow starters. This doesn't mean something wonderful isn't brewing inside.

The student's pediatrician can tell you the average ages that children pass through various stages of physical coordination.[3] The Infinity Walk motor pattern can be useful for all children who are neurologically mature enough to walk up and down stairs with alternating leg movements. Of course, we would not expect younger children's brains to be ready to learn the more advanced forms of Infinity Walk. All adults who feel uncoordinated can greatly benefit from the Infinity Walk Sensorimotor Program.

2. **THERE ARE LARGE DISCREPANCIES IN THE STUDENT'S ABILITIES; STUDENT APPEARS BRIGHTER THAN HE OR SHE TESTS**

The most dramatic results with my work have occurred with students thought to be brighter than they tested. These children are usually missing a single link in how their otherwise very competent brains work. Like train tracks with a missing rail, the problem can appear very serious. However, this problem vanishes when the brain develops the missing link that is needed for more complete brain communication and cooperation. Once resolved, the train system can operate immediately as if there never were a problem. This missing link is often one dominant sense (vision or hearing) that is not sharing the same hemisphere with the other sense and/or motor control center.

Large discrepancies in abilities tell me these students have good minds and the motivation to develop the parts of their brains that they have been able to access. Once they learn to access more of the brain, these students are dynamite! Unfortunately, they are sometimes labeled underachievers. This comes from a logic that says, "If they do so well in a subject they like, they simply aren't trying hard enough in the other subjects." Nonsense. *It is human nature to explore wherever the door is open and a path has been laid. The appearance of lack of interest should be an immediate indicator that the student has not found easy access to exploring the material.*

---

[3] Also see Cherry, C., Godwin, D., and Staples, J., "Processes of Child Development," in *Is the Left Brain Always Right?* Belmont, CA: Fearon Teacher Aids, 1989.

In fact, I consider it a sign of health to follow an open pathway and excel in that area, rather than continually fail at breaking through a closed route. In the long run, these children may be happier and better adjusted than those who want to please an adult so much that they use up their energies on tasks neurologically unavailable to them. I would much rather see them developing their own special talents that can provide them with a lifetime of self-esteem. Fortunately, the results of the Infinity Walk program strongly suggest that these students don't have to limit their successes to one area. New neurological paths can be opened.[4]

3. **STUDENT DEVELOPS UNUSUAL VISUAL COMPENSATIONS FOR READING**

   **MOVES HEAD INSTEAD OF EYES WHEN READING**

   **PLACES READING OR WRITING MATERIAL TO FAR LEFT OR FAR RIGHT**

   **ALWAYS TILTS HEAD TO SIDE WHEN READING OR WRITING**

   **EYES HAVE A SPACEY LOOK, OR GET TIRED QUICKLY WHEN READING**

   **FALLS ASLEEP WHEN TRYING TO READ MORE THAN A FEW PAGES**

These are all indicators that left and right hemispheres are not yet sufficiently networked to allow optimal visual (sensory) cooperation when reading. When we look left, the right hemisphere is dominating our visual task; when we look right, the left hemisphere takes greater responsibility for visually absorbing the information. As our eyes scan a page from left to right there is a moment when the hemispheres must smoothly cooperate in the giving and taking of leadership in order for the reading not to suffer. *Without well coordinated visual input between the two hemispheres, language and math symbols can be lost or confused, resulting in diminished comprehension.*

Students who do not move their eyes when reading are avoiding hemispheric cooperation by either moving the book or their heads, or by placing the book to their far left or far right. Unknowingly, they are showing excellent compensation. However, the long-term price may be unnecessary stress and

---

[4] Three UCLA researchers have determined that the dendrites in the brain actually grow longer the more they are used. Learning something new creates an anatomical change in dendrite connections in less than a minute! See the January 1993 issue of *The Journal of Comparative Neurology* for more information. Cited from interview with Dr. Robert Jacobs in *The Daily Breeze,* January 13, 1993.

strain, headaches, or the feeling that nothing ever comes easily. Tired, sore eyes and the quick onset of exhaustion (sometimes mistaken as lack of motivation) are all indicators of the internal strain these students experience when trying to gain hemispheric visual cooperation.

The cocking of the head when concentrating on reading, writing, drawing, or trying to comprehend something can look cute on a young child. However, this gesture is the sign of a very specific problem in the older child, which, if not resolved, can lead to muscular imbalances and neck pain as an adult. Why do some people tilt their heads when performing certain tasks? The eye that is placed higher by the tilting gains greater dominance power. I've seen students tilt their heads left to strengthen right-eye dominated reading. Then, they will tilt their heads right when they change the task to drawing, allowing them better access to right brain abilities through the left eye! This is a wonderful compensation, and a short-term solution to a less than fully integrated brain. Long term, it may cause more physical pain than it was worth. Greater integration of visual sensory input from both hemispheres can eliminate all these problems.

The solution to these visual compensations is not to stop students from doing them. They wouldn't be doing them if they didn't need to. The solution is to help them develop visual hemispheric cooperation through the Infinity Walk program, so the need to tilt their heads can drop away naturally. The sections in chapter 11 on visual/spatial and verbal/linguistic intelligences would be most helpful.

## 4. STUDENT HAS UNUSUAL WAY OF WRITING THE NUMBER EIGHT

People who find it impossible to write the number eight as one continuous flowing line are demonstrating how difficult it is for their sensorimotor nerves to support each other across the hemispheres.

The "8" (as well as the infinity sign) is a perfect symbol to exercise left-right integration. Young children who have not completed the neurological development needed for easy fine motor cooperation between hemispheres find it impossible to continually reverse directions without getting lost. As they draw, they begin by creating the equivalent of an "S," and then a mirror image S, but starting from bottom up, making it in the child's mind an upside down, backwards S. Try this with a dark magic marker on white paper. Watch your progress through the back of the paper, as you turn your S's in three dimensional space, to create an 8 as a child would first learn it. It will give you a whole new respect for your own mastery of our very complex system of symbolic language. Some young children's solution to the puzzle of the 8 is two circles, one on top of the other, both drawn in the same direction, clockwise or counterclockwise. Another, much rarer compensation is drawing a 3, and then a reversed 3 to complete filling in the two open spaces remaining on the left side. Both these methods avoid the sensorimotor hemispheric integration needed to complete the number eight as one flowing line. Learning the Infinity Walk Sensorimotor Pattern corrects this problem. Once children can walk an eight pattern, they can also draw it.

(This method can also help in learning to print other numbers and letters. Have the child walk behind you as you walk the shape of the symbol until they can walk it alone. Once they can create the shape through the motor action of their legs it will be much easier for them to create the symbols on paper through the motor action of their hands.)

## 5. STUDENT READS WITH POOR COMPREHENSION
### READS WITH POETIC, FLOWING STYLE, BUT COMPREHENSION IS POOR
### LABORS AT READING ONE WORD AT A TIME WITH POOR COMPREHENSION
### COMPREHENSION IS LOST WHEN READING OUT LOUD

The tendency to read sentences as a string of short choppy isolated sounds is like not seeing the forest for the trees. The spoken word units are not allowed to flow into a melody of expressive speech, and the meaning of the reading is lost in the focus on the individual words. This inability to create these strings of sounds into meaningful content is also reflected in monotone speech when reading. The student who overly focuses on detail misses out on the revelation that the beauty of the forest can be greater than the simple sum of each tree. This linear/sequential view of the world is indicative of too great a reliance on beta type rules.

Students who read well out loud but can't tell you what they just read are seeing and expressing the forest, but missing the details called trees. Some alpha/theta type students read so well out loud that teachers may not be quick to realize that they are treating the written word as a musical or artistic expression and are not tuning in to the content of the reading. Absorbing content would require them to focus attention on the meaning of the individual words, which does not come naturally to these people. The same problem can be seen in students who treat writing assignments like an art project. They focus more on the flow of lines on the page, than on the content the lines represent. Whether a student overly focuses on the trees or the forest, comprehension can be greatly improved through the visual/spatial and verbal/linguistic phases of the Infinity Walk program. (See pages 143-147 and 148-155).

### 6. STUDENT TENDS TO CROSS ARMS OR LEGS WHEN READING, TALKING, OR CONCENTRATING

The crossing of the left and right sides of the body is an indication of unconscious wisdom trying to get the two sides working together better. What can't be joined easily through the corpus callosum, the natural link between left and right hemispheres in the brain, is attempted through linking the limbs. There is no solid evidence that I know of to suggest this is more than a body gesture of support or security. However, the nervous system is an amazing, adaptable life force. I would not prematurely reject the possibility that this posturing may somehow energize the two hemispheres through the increased neurological response to touch. This in fact is a theory within the field of applied kinesiology. For now, though, I don't suggest discouraging someone from crossing limbs when concentrating, or from any other seemingly idiosyncratic posture. Our inner wisdom knows what we need to help us through difficult times. This need will resolve itself once the brain hemispheres are more fully cooperating.

### 7. STUDENT READS BACKWARDS (RIGHT TO LEFT) FASTER OR MORE EASILY THAN FORWARD

The left to right flow of our written English language was designed for the right eye dominant person. The dominant right eye reaches across to the left side of the page, locks on to the first word on the line, and scans easily across the line, from left to right. In fact, the right eye's control over the visual information grows even stronger as it scans toward the right side of the page. Try this with your own reading right now. Read this line of text while being very aware of how your right eye moves over into the left eye's territory and then scans back into its own comfortable territory on the right side of the page.

This explanation may not make sense to you if you are left eye dominant for reading. One of the proofreaders for *Infinity Walk* kept asking me to rewrite the previous paragraph until we realized that even though she tests as right eye dominant, she has a chronic habit of cocking her head when reading, so her left eye becomes dominant for reading. Patricia was one of those precocious preschoolers who starts reading at age three. Her visual compensation is probably left over from her early start on comprehending two-dimensional symbols.

The right eye dominant person is greatly advantaged in reading for another reason. The center for verbal language expression is almost always located in the left hemisphere. This creates an ease between reading and being able to communicate what has been read. The left eye dominant person may need to work harder to develop this skill.

Let's look at what happens when a left eye dominant person reads. The dominant left eye begins reading the line from its own territory on the left side of the page, but quickly loses its edge as its line of vision begins to cross the bridge of the nose and moves into the right eye's territory. Each eye naturally wants to command the input coming in from its side of the head, so the right eye adds to the struggle and confusion at this point. People with this neurological pattern sometimes start out reading strong, but seem to lose confidence around the middle of the written line.

This does not mean that all left eye dominant people had difficulty learning to read. There are many ways to compensate neurologically. Many left eye dominant people who are also good readers (like Patricia) have learned to switch eye dominance, or have developed extreme visual vigilance. The "switchers" often seem to have two characteristics: sometimes intense in their visual observations, other times seemingly totally unaware of their surrounding circumstances. Some, who forced their dominant left eye to master written language through concentration and vigilant self-monitoring of their reading, may appear to have an overly intense and sometimes nervous personality.

In contrast, the left eye dominant people who did not strive to master written language may have preserved more of their visual connection to the alpha and theta realms, giving them other talents and abilities. Patricia tells me that she has absolutely no ability for drawing; a small sacrifice for her early development of two-dimensional language abilities.

The reason some people can read backwards more confidently may make a little more sense now. Reading from right to left for a left eye dominant person, is what a right eye dominant person would experience reading left to right.

### TESTING FOR READING BACKWARDS, AND A SOLUTION

To test a left eye dominant person's ability to read without the handicap of left to right scanning I suggest you have them read sentences in reverse, from right to left. Many will lose the handicap while reading and pick up speed and accuracy. The following paragraph is an example of right to left scanning, and can usually be read with greater ease by left eye dominant people than right eye dominant people. (Many left eye dominant people can also read mirror-image writing, as did Leonardo da Vinci. I don't encourage this because it can confuse the order of letters in spelling words.) When you are working with students, be sure to create a sample paragraph suitable to their reading level for word recognition.

(begin here)

read people Some .easy feels it when fun be can Reading
by faster read to learn can You .others than faster
a Pick .forwards then and backwards reading practicing
the reading by Start .reading in interested are you book
you this do To .backwards sentence first the in words
begin and sentence the of word last the find to need
time this but, again sentence same the read Next .there
sentence any read normally would you way the it read
a this practice you If .right to left from it Read
faster reading yourself find will you, day each little
the remember still can you that notice also may You
reading were you though even, read you what of content
book a in backwards read you when, Obviously .faster
the of meaning the understand always not will you,
.also backwards be will words the because sentence
your improve still will book a in backwards Reading
the understand don't you if even, skills reading
from, time second the for it read you until content
.right to left

(end)

Left eye dominant students who have given up on reading can be given a second chance to enjoy written language by challenging them to read backwards from their textbook as fast as they can. Since the words will not form a logical sentence when reading from right to left, this also takes off the pressure of needing to understand what they are reading. Reading in reverse can help them to see each word as a separate unit. This is particularly helpful to students who tend to miss words when reading. Reading the sentence in reverse before reading it forward is like unscrambling a puzzle. Students get curious about what the sentence really means. Most important, it's a fun way to learn.

If some of these seven indicators of less than optimal sensorimotor integration sound like you or someone you know, there is hope! They are positive signs that a present learning difficulty may be much simpler than it has seemed.

## PART 3

# Walking the Path to Unlimited Potential

*Photo courtesy of Patricia Anne Jacobs*

# CHAPTER 10

# The Infinity Walk: A Progressive Sensorimotor Program

**B**efore taking you through Infinity Walk, I'd like to remind you that profound change never occurs in the starkness of technique alone. The foundation of great change within ourselves is always built on the maturation of self-empowering beliefs; a growing awareness that we do not have to live our lives the way they were handed to us. The more we understand the dynamics of our miraculous brains, the easier it is to let go of limited programmed thinking and accept our minds' infinite potential. For this reason, I believe a thorough understanding of Part I and Part II of this book is important before one can master Infinity Walk. Whether you are entering into this program for yourself, or in order to teach it to others, it is essential that a fascination for the unique potential of each mind is first established before proceeding to Infinity Walk.

## ESSENTIAL STEPS TO NATURAL LEARNING

#1    Part I      Empowering Self-Beliefs

#2    Part II     Facilitating Self-Understanding

#3    Part III    Self-Paced Training in Infinity Walk

Now, what exactly is Infinity Walk? *Infinity Walk is my name for a sequence of progressively more complex challenges to our sensory and motor nervous system.* It starts with the development and refinement of motor coordination across both brain hemispheres, while improving body image and kinèsthetic (movement) awareness. This integration of the muscular system is a necessary foundation for the demonstration of all types of learning. Without a hemispherically integrated motor nervous system we are unable to fully express our intelligence and creativity.

To this motor foundation, progressive training in the six additional types of sensory intelligences that Howard Gardner has identified is added.[1] Each type of sensory intelligence must be expressed through the motor nervous system. Developing these various sensory abilities while doing the Infinity Walk is the most powerful way I know of to increase one's natural capacities in every area of interest. For the child, it becomes a fun game of "How many things can you do at once?" — totally separate from the stress of academic performance. For the aspiring adult, it becomes a means of opening the mind to cognitive and creative excellence.

## APPLYING INFINITY WALK TO HOWARD GARDNER'S MULTIPLE INTELLIGENCES THEORY

| Types of Intelligences | Areas Needing Training |
|---|---|
| 1. Body/Kinesthetic (foundation of Infinity Walk) | motor nervous system<br>both hemispheres; beta |

*Add the following to the Walk:*

| | |
|---|---|
| 2. Visual/Spatial | 3-D visual imaging<br>3-D spatial perception<br>more right hemisphere; alpha |
| 3. Verbal/ Linguistic | consistent 2-D recognition<br>attention span for 2-D world<br>more left hemisphere, beta;<br>combining 2-D and 3-D<br>left and right hemisphere; beta and alpha |

---

[1] Gardner, H. *Frames of Mind: The Theory of Multiple Intelligences.* New York: Basic Books, 1983. Gardner, H. *Multiple Intelligences: The Theory in Practice.* New York: Basic Books, 1993. Lazear, David. *Seven Ways of Knowing: Understanding Multiple Intelligences.* Palatine, Illinois, 1991.

| Types of Intelligences | Areas Needing Training |
|---|---|
| 4.  Musical/Rhythmic | inner timing<br>mood and motivation from music<br>mostly right hemisphere;<br>beta, alpha, theta, depending on music-inducing mood<br><br>also left hemisphere, beta if using words or motor sequencing |
| 5.  Interpersonal | effective communication<br>motor nerves of speech muscles<br>both hemispheres<br>beta and alpha, with strong auditory<br>also theta if deeply emotional |
| 6.  Logical/Mathematical | objective reasoning skills<br>abstract understanding<br>"order out of chaos"<br>both hemispheres,<br>beta and alpha, strong visual |
| 7.  Intrapersonal | self-awareness and insight<br>philosophical understanding<br>integrated body/mind/emotions<br>both hemispheres, all senses<br>beta, alpha and theta |

# HOW AND WHY INFINITY WALK WORKS

The principle behind Infinity Walk is quite simple. The brain and nervous system will respond to training just as a muscle will respond to exercise. It would be silly for someone with poor muscle tone and little muscle strength to enter a weight lifting competition. This person would be doomed to failure and public embarrassment. However, this is what we do when we expect our minds to perform any complex task before we are neurologically prepared. Neurological preparation does not mean drilling at a particular topic until it finally makes sense to us. Drilling at a task does not teach the task, it only indicates how closely we are approximating the correct behavior each time we attempt it. *It's important to realize that traditional education was never intended to be a program to neurologically prepare us for learning.* Traditional education was set up as a system to constantly test us on materials that have been assigned to us to learn. (Progressive school programs across the country are beginning to change this with more focus on *how* to learn.[2])

The purpose of Infinity Walk is very different from traditional education, though it can lead to success in school. Infinity Walk is a method of developing increasingly more sophisticated neural networking in the brain that, in turn, will increase or free our natural ability to learn anything. Trying to learn something new can be like trying to walk through a door without opening it. In this same way, a neurological pathway must be created before we can expect to retain or apply new learnings. Expecting success before this neurological doorway is opened can only lead to frustration and embarrassment. Make a promise to yourself that any time you or students you are working with are having difficulty learning something, you will immediately stop trying to force the information through a closed door and return to the Infinity Walk program.

Each person starts Infinity Walk at their present level of neurological mastery and progresses toward excellence in whatever area of learning they wish to master. Just as a well planned exercise program will always lead to better body tone, coordination, and muscle strength, neurological mastery is inevitable with proper training (given no prior permanent neurological damage).

In addition to Infinity Walk's value in preparing us to learn, it can be used by people of all ages to balance the emotions, by calming the overanxious and stimulating the under-energized, bored, and depressed. I've even seen it help people break through to unconscious memories that have held them back from being the best they can be.

---

[2] Much has been written on improving education in the United States. I could not list all of them but the following is a good start. Toch, Thomas. *In the Name of Excellence: The Struggle to Reform the Nation's Schools.* New York: Oxford University Press, 1991. Seymour, Daniel and Terry. *America's Best Classrooms.* Princeton, NJ: Peterson's Guide, 1992. Sadker, Myra and David. Failing at Fairness: *How America's Schools Cheat Girls.* New York: Charles Scribner, 1993. Gatek, Gerald. Education in the U.S. Englewood Cliffs, NJ: Prentice Hall, 1988.

Guides to help parents get the most out of the United States' current educational system are also flourishing. Nemko, Martin. *How to Get Your Child a Private School Education in a Public School.* Berkeley, CA: Ten Speed Press, 1989. Nicoll, Vivienne and Wilkie, Lyn. *Literacy at Home and School: A Guide for Parents.* Rozelle, Australia: Primary English Teaching Association, 1991. Pierce, Ronald K. *What Are We Really Trying to Teach Anyway?* A Father's Focus on School Reform. San Francisco, CA: Center for Self-Governance, 1993.

Walked briskly at an aerobic pace, Infinity Walk can also add cardiovascular exercise to its already numerous neurological benefits. Although Infinity Walk was not developed as a physical exercise, it has proven to be especially valuable to people confined indoors due to poor health, injury, or bad weather. Miles can be walked on a flat comfortable surface without you ever having to leave your home. Let's look at how all this is accomplished.

To the degree that any part of our sensory and motor nervous system does not function or cooperate with the rest of our brain, we are handicapped. Most of us compensate so well over time that we are rarely challenged to overcome these handicaps after the early school years. Whatever we did well at during the school years became a part of our lives and enhanced our self-esteem. Whatever we failed to master was hidden away in the darkest corners of our past, under the label of "Embarrassing moments we would rather forget."

Unfortunately, this approach to preserving our self-esteem takes away any opportunity to develop the needed neural pathways to perform these and other related tasks easily. Under the guise of personal likes and dislikes, we box ourselves into stagnant attitudes and habits, and they trick us into believing that we have chosen our limited reality, or that change is undesirable or impossible.

Motivated students who have completed the Infinity Walk program have much higher self-esteem, and a thorough understanding of how to use their bodies and minds to excel at anything. Their standardized test scores confirm that major progress has been made on a cognitive level as well. Take a look at these pre- and post- Woodcock test scores from a 7-session summer group I worked with recently.[3]

# WOODCOCK READING MASTERY SCORES BEFORE AND AFTER INFINITY WALK

All testing by Shelly Hassall, N.Y.S. Cert., Special Education (8 students, ages 10 to 16, tested 6/93 and 10/93)

---

[3] This group was composed of students from Rochester, New York. All students were obtained on a volunteer basis through the local Learning Disabilities Association. Students were selected on the basis of motivation and the "classroom clues to sensorimotor blocks" found in chapter 9. Parents were involved in the program and attended each session.

## VISUAL-AUDITORY LEARNING (READING READINESS)

| Actual Grade | Pre-test grade level | Post-test grade level |
|---|---|---|
| 4.9 | K.8 | 15.3 |
| 5.9 | 3.0 | 11.3 |
| 5.9 | 6.2 | 16.9 |
| 5.9 | 11.3 | 16.9 |
| 5.9 | 15.3 | 16.9 |
| 9.9 | 6.2 | 11.3 |
| 10.9 | 5.0 | 16.9 |
| 10.9 | 16.9 | 16.9 |

16.9 highest possible score
(last year of college)

## WORD IDENTIFICATION (VISUAL, PHONETIC AND RISK-TAKING)

| Actual grade | Pre-test grade level | Post-test grade level |
|---|---|---|
| 4.9 | 2.5 | 3.2 |
| 5.9 | 4.0 | 4.1 |
| 5.9 | 6.1 | 8.1 |
| 5.9 | 4.4 | 4.0 |
| 5.9 | 7.1 | 7.8 |
| 9.9 | 12.9 | 16.3 |
| 10.9 | 8.7 | 13.5 |
| 10.9 | 8.1 | 12.0 |

## WORD COMPREHENSION

| Actual Grade | Pre-test Grade Level | Post-test Grade Level |
| --- | --- | --- |
| 4.9 | 3.0 | 5.7 |
| 5.9 | 3.8 | 6.6 |
| 5.9 | 6.1 | 9.7 |
| 5.9 | 4.9 | 5.2 |
| 5.9 | 4.5 | 11.7 |
| 9.9 | 16.9 | 16.9 |
| 10.9 | 10.4 | 12.9 |
| 10.9 | 16.6 | 16.9 |

## READING PASSAGE COMPREHENSION

| Actual Grade | Pre-test Grade Level | Post-test Grade Level |
| --- | --- | --- |
| 4.9 | 2.3 | 3.3 |
| 5.9 | 3.9 | 4.9 |
| 5.9 | 7.9 | 16.5 |
| 5.9 | 4.2 | 3.5 |
| 5.9 | 4.2 | 8.4 |
| 9.9 | 16.9 | 16.9 |
| 10.9 | 7.9 | 12.9 |
| 10.9 | 15.6 | 16.9 |

Infinity Walk was intentionally developed to encourage the neurological preparation we need to overcome any learning block involving sensory or motor nerves, as well as to help free us from limiting attitudes, beliefs, and habits. This is why Infinity Walk can be equally helpful to a child labeled learning disabled as it can be to a dancer, or a college student, or a housewife trying to get up the courage to take the first step toward joining the professional world.

## Pre-Test for the Body/Kinesthetic Foundation of Infinity Walk

Let's take advantage of this moment as the perfect opportunity for you to notice how your body and motor nervous system would naturally do Infinity Walk. I'm going to ask you to not read further until you walk around the room you are in, creating the pattern of the number eight on the floor. The pattern needs to be about 8 to 10 feet long for an adult, and 5 to 8 feet long for a child. Repeat the pattern a few times until you are satisfied with the shape of the imaginary eight that you are creating with your footsteps.

PLEASE STOP READING NOW AND WALK THE FIGURE EIGHT PATTERN

DON'T SKIP THIS PART — IT IS IMPOSSIBLE TO IMAGINE IN SUFFICIENT DETAIL HOW YOU WILL DO THIS. ONCE YOU READ THE NEXT SECTION, THE OPPORTUNITY WILL BE GONE FOREVER.

## The First Assessment of Your Natural Motor Coordination

Now, let's make a few mental or written notes about your experience before going on.

1.  Were you able to walk the eight pattern without hesitation? (Don't be concerned if you had trouble with the pattern. Later, I'll show you how to neurologically build up to walking it perfectly.)
2.  Did you feel the need to look at the floor to create the pattern?
3.  How balanced and even was the pattern? Were the two circles that make up the eight pattern the same size and shape?
4.  What were your arms doing while you were walking? Did they hang limp? Were they bent at your elbows and held against your body? Were they relaxed and swinging at your sides? If they were swinging, did they have a rhythm to

their swing? Did your arms swing forward with the same-sided leg, or with the opposite-sided leg? Did they swing just in front of you or also behind?

5.  How did you feel about yourself as you walked the eight pattern? Did you feel confident, confused, athletic, awkward? Did you have any awareness of yourself at all, or were you completely occupied with the task?

Keep your answers to these questions in mind as I take you through the basic pattern for Infinity Walk. This pattern will be the foundation on which we build all the sensory and motor networking and cooperation needed for all types of intelligences and creativity.

## DEVELOPING BODY/KINESTHETIC INTELLIGENCE

I'll first talk you through the basic motor pattern for Infinity Walk, and then explain how this pattern neurologically affects us. For those who have a strong athletic or formal dance background the basic pattern may seem too simple to have any value, but this is far from the case. Many people have some difficulty with the basic walk the first time they try it. Others may think it is easy until they try to add sensory challenges to the Walk. You can quickly fan the kineograph images that start on this page with your thumb to see how the basic pattern looks in motion. The eight pattern, the foundation for Infinity Walk, is by itself a complex demonstration of motor nerve integration and cooperation. To it, we will add further motor complexity as well as a full program of sensory and cognitive tasks, which will enhance the remaining six types of multiple intelligences.[4]

Take a minute to practice walking the eight pattern that you experimented with in the pre-test. If you find it difficult to walk in an eight pattern, try these suggestions first:

*Draw an eight on paper first, imagining that you are walking around it as you draw it.*

*Place a chair at the center of each circle that make up the two ends of the eight. Use them as a reminder of your eight pattern on the floor as you walk around them.*

---

[4] Actually, Gardner himself does not believe we are limited to just seven types of intelligences. However, since his earlier work on the topic, the concept has met with such popularity that I decided to organize the exercises in this manner, since it is familiar to so many educators. See Gardner's forward in David Lazear's *Seven Ways of Knowing* (Palatine, Illinois: Skylight Publishing, 1991) for Gardner's explanation.

*Place small objects on the floor to indicate the pathway of the eight pattern. (Remove all visual props as soon as you are able to visualize the eight pattern on the floor.)*

Once you are sure of your eight pattern, improve it by making the eight a smooth, flowing movement with balance and proportion between its two looping halves. Next, add a natural, comfortable swing to your arms as you walk. Each arm should swing forward as your OPPOSITE leg steps forward. If you find it difficult to continue swinging your arms as you walk the eight pattern, try this. As you walk, touch the front of the upper thigh of your right leg with your left hand. On the next step, touch your left thigh with your right hand. Continue touching alternating thighs as you walk. Touching your thigh with your opposite hand establishes extra nerve communication that can help your body remember which arm and leg are to move together. You may wish to practice this "opposite thigh touch" movement while walking in a straight line before trying it with the eight pattern.

This movement of opposing limbs (arm with opposite leg) is a sign that the motor nerves in the two hemispheres of your brain are working together and in cooperation with each other. Many highly-compensating adults as well as children with learning difficulties have not developed this alternating, rhythmic movement of opposing limbs as part of their natural walk.

Let's take a minute to understand why the development of the opposing limb movement is so important. Our ability to make any movement with any part of our body depends on the motor nervous system, and how well it is integrated with the rest of our brain. All movement and sensory awareness on the right side of our bodies is controlled by the motor nerves and sensory nerves coming from the left hemisphere of our brains. The converse is true for the left side of our bodies. This is just the way we are created. The two hemispheres of our brains have the ability to operate somewhat independently of each other. They also communicate with each other across the corpus callosum, a rather complicated bunch of nerve fibers that runs across the middle of our brain, attaching the left and right hemispheres.

When this nerve bridge is surgically cut (in rare severe cases of epilepsy), both sides of the body continue to operate, but separately. They lose their capacity to work together or to even know what the other side is doing.[5] This lack of cooperation can

---

[5] Ornstein, Robert, and Thompson, Richard. "The Divided Brain," in *The Amazing Brain*. Boston: Houghton Mifflin Company, 1984.

create all kinds of handicaps and differences in perceptions. For instance, physical coordination between our two sides is lost. Something seen out of the corner of our right eye will only elicit a response from the left side of our brain (and the right side of our body). The left side of our body will be confused as to why the right side is reacting. The inability to take in the whole circumstances of any given situation can create anxiety that leads to vigilant behavior. Imagine what it would be like to try to copy down a telephone number with your right hand while you are looking at the number out of the corner of your left eye, without any way to neurologically communicate between your left eye and your right hand. It would be impossible.

Certainly, having a severed corpus callosum could be quite a disadvantage to learning and communicating. What you probably have never realized is that almost all of us are handicapped to some degree by this inability to communicate across the hemispheres, not because our corpus callosum has been severed, but because we have not fully developed the neurological networking abilities that are a natural gift of our genetics. Why haven't we? Because in the past, learning has been evaluated on mastering specific bits of information rather than on developing our brains to their greatest potential. This leaves us with an odd assortment of knowledge and skills with lots of "holes" in our neurological network.

## Hemispheric Motor Cooperation

Now let's look at the basic motor pattern for the Infinity Walk in more detail. As our opposing limbs move forward, both hemispheres of our brains work together simultaneously to create a perfectly synchronized movement between our arm and leg. Then, as the moving leg touches the floor, our weight shifts in order to bring the second leg forward and take the next step. At this moment, the hemisphere in charge of moving our leg forward must shift its control away from the leg and toward the same-sided arm that will need to swing forward during the next step.

Simultaneously, this same hemisphere must give control of walking and balance to the other hemisphere. In order to maintain perfect flow and coordination through the full movement, each hemisphere must give up control as the other side takes over the responsibility for the next step or arm swing. This give-and-take of control between the two hemispheres must be done with perfect precision and timing. Without the  complete cooperation of the full brain, we can end up feeling uncoordinated or slow in movement (and motor generated speech).

All of us accomplished the alternating leg movement when we first learned to walk. Whether we mastered this movement sequence with grace and style is another story all together. However, many of us never went on to add the more neurologically sophisticated swinging of opposing arms as we walk. What does this mean neurologically? It means we learned to alternate brain dominance for a single isolated movement (in this case, moving our legs forward), but did not learn to assign simultaneous dominance to our two hemispheres for two different tasks (moving opposing arm and leg). When moving opposing arms and legs, both hemispheres must stay active and dominant for different tasks but be willing at a moment's notice to exchange the task for which they are dominant — without losing a beat!

When should we have naturally learned such a sophisticated movement? Developmentally, we would have learned this movement before we learned to walk. Advanced crawling actually requires this movement, especially if we are trying to quickly glide across the floor. Without the movement of opposing limbs while crawling, we would have to lift the same-sided hand and leg off the floor at the same time. This is a much less stable movement than lifting one limb from each side and then alternating the pair of limbs.

So don't all babies crawl before they walk? Why do so many people lack this level of neurological sophistication? I can't say why you or someone you know may not have developed a strong natural opposing limb walk yet, but I can suggest a theory. Some infants may have been confined to such small areas, like playpens, that they never developed the incentive to master the subtle complexities of a more advanced, opposing limb crawl. If you, as an adult, lived in a very small room, would you bother swinging your arms as you crossed the room? Babies who master the opposing limb crawl can pick up so much speed in their movements that parents must watch them every moment. So, parents naturally want to confine them to smaller safer areas. Hopefully, understanding the importance of longer distance speed crawling will encourage parents to give their infants more supervised crawling time.

Another reason the opposite limb movement may not feel natural or happen automatically when you walk is that it may not have been practiced after you started walking. Children who are overly praised for being quiet, not running, and controlling their body movements become inhibited in the free use of their bodies. This habit can continue throughout their lives until they intentionally strengthen the necessary neuro-motor patterns for larger, more spontaneous body movement. Active sports, dance, and the martial arts, as well as the Infinity Walk program, can help overcome emotionally-based motor inhibition.

Let's go back to your own basic pattern of walking the Infinity Walk, and refine it a little more. Encourage your arms to swing forward with the same amount of movement as your legs. If you are walking slowly, your arm movement is smaller, slower, more graceful. If you are walking briskly, your arms will pick up the same amount of speed, and swing forward and backward a little farther. The feeling will be more athletic. Let each arm swing forward and backward with equal strength and determination. Begin to encourage your arms to swing from your shoulders rather than from your elbows.

You may need to free up your shoulder blades a little, through some stretching exercises, if you have a tendency to hold them tight. Watch a cat or dog walk to get an idea of the flow of perfect movement. Notice how each step involves the entire limb, right up though the animal's shoulders and hips. You can actually see their backs twist and roll in perfect rhythm with their walk. This is the perfect freedom of movement that comes from complete neurological integration and cooperation, and it's possible in all mammals, including humans.

How about the loops on your basic eight pattern? What happens to your arms? Do they slow down as you walk around one of the curves? Does one or both of them stop for a moment? Do you lose your opposing limb rhythm? Does this part of the walking pattern feel less graceful, or less secure, or less powerful? Do any of these things happen as you walk around one end of the eight more than at the other end?

Notice that while walking the eight pattern you are alternating between making a left turn, and making a right turn. This is another hemispheric dominance change, as if you didn't have enough happening already! Every time our two brain hemispheres change dominance as we reverse the direction of our walking, it is possible for our brains to "short circuit" for a moment while we figure out the give-and-take of how to go about making this change. This makes the turns on the eight pattern more neurologically complex than just walking a straight line. We can observe with great accuracy the exact moment of this short circuit by paying attention to our bodies as we walk this basic pattern. I'll explain how to do this later.

Another point of possible confusion comes as our walk straightens out after we finish coming around one of the curves and walk toward the middle of the eight. For the few moments that we are walking in a straight line, our two hemispheres are attempting to share dominance over our walk. However, this moment of equally shared dominance is short-lived. As we near the crossing point of the two circles another  battle starts between the two hemispheres. One hemisphere wants to continue walking in the circle it had been in charge of, while the other hemisphere wants to continue walking straight. This middle point of the eight seems to create a high degree of neurological confusion in people who have not yet mastered neurological cooperation across their hemispheres. This confusion in our brains is easily detectable by noticing our bodies get confused at different points while walking the eight pattern. Fortunately, our nervous system learns very quickly when we provide it with new information and new experiences, at a reasonable pace.

## Looking For "Short Circuits"

As you add more neurological complexity to Infinity Walk, you will be able to determine how fast to proceed through the program by noticing the quality of the basic eight walking pattern. As you observe someone (or yourself) walking in an eight pattern be aware that the left side of the body, including the left side of the head, the left facial expression, and the left eye and ear, are operating off the right brain hemisphere, and vice versa. This is true for any motor function, and predominantly true for any sensory function. Also remember that for most people the language communication center is in the left hemisphere, and therefore can be observed through the right side of their bodies. Therefore, when we see someone lose the rhythm of the arm swing on the right side, but never in the left arm, we know that the task they are doing just overloaded the left hemisphere. We know this because when a hemisphere overloads it will cut back on the less essential tasks in order to have more neural energy to attempt the new request. If this electrical overload is extreme, we will probably also see the person stop walking.

This type of short circuit may also happen when emotions are involved. Trying to keep performance anxiety, embarrassment, and feelings of inadequacy hidden while performing a motor or cognitive task requires a tremendous amount of neural energy. Since the brain will prioritize messages of anxiety as a survival concern, people who try to suppress emotions rarely have sufficient neural energy left over for sophisticated muscle movement. Their movements may be less frequent, smaller, or lacking in flow or grace. Fortunately, Infinity Walk can also help remedy this.

If a total motor shutdown occurs in someone you are working with while walking the eight pattern (they stop walking as well as swinging their arms) the overload may also be triggering feelings of embarrassment, failure, or fear. Be aware of this, so you can help redirect this person away from their self-consciousness. Needless to say, never allow an onlooker to make fun of someone who is just learning the basic Infinity Walk pattern.

It would be best not to attempt the more complex Infinity Walk patterns presented at the end of this chapter until the basic eight pattern feels comfortable to you, and you can walk at least 10 minutes of the pattern without losing your arm swing at any point. Creating quality in the movement is more important neurologically than trying to prematurely add the advanced exercises to the program. In the beginning try to walk the eight pattern more than once a day. Remember, you are creating new communication pathways in your brain. This takes remarkably little time and effort, but is does take some daily practice. Most people who could not walk the basic motor pattern in a pre-test were able to walk it smoothly within a week, as long as they practiced daily. Don't be discouraged if it takes you longer. Once you have it mastered, you'll pick up speed quickly with the rest of the program. If you are in the opposite position of feeling this program may be too simple for you, wait awhile; your time will come!

If you have a particular interest in perfecting the motor nerve balance between the two sides of your body, here are some things to look for while walking the basic pattern:

- Arms swing evenly and in the direction you are walking

- Arms continue swinging throughout the entire basic walk

- Arm movement is from shoulders, rather than from elbows

- Arms' range of motion while swinging is equal in front of and behind your body (forward and backward swing)

- Shoulders are flexible and relaxed, rather than rigid

- Shoulders are even; one is not held higher than the other

- Hands are relaxed open, but not limp

- Any elbow movement is the same for both arms

- Elbows are not rigidly straight or overly bent

- Breathing is comfortable and continuous

- Back is relaxed so breath expands rib cage on both sides and across the back, as well as expanding out the front

- Each foot is placed solidly on the floor, with heel touching first, followed by each foot rolling firmly onto the ball of the foot before leaving the floor again

- All five toes of each foot gently press the floor as each foot rolls forward in preparation for the next step

- Both feet point in the direction you are walking, as you take each step

- Knees are gently relaxed to cushion the impact of each foot making contact with the floor, giving the sense of floating or flowing as you walk
- Neck, forehead, eyes, jaw, throat, and tongue are relaxed

This may seem like a tremendous amount to pay attention to, but with time, it can become second nature. The payoff of learning to move with such a high degree of neurological awareness will greatly outweigh your initial effort. This fine tuning of your motor nervous system can create a sense of presence that exudes confidence and ease with yourself.

In sum, the increased movement awareness and coordination that are possible through this basic motor walk is a very important foundation for Infinity Walk. Even as your training progresses through the six types of sensory intelligences, it would be highly advantageous to continue to refine the basic walk. Once in a while, go back over the list of reminders in this chapter to be sure you are continuing to gain neurological sophistication in motor or movement integration.

## Upgrading the Motor Complexity of Infinity Walk

Once you have integrated Infinity Walk's body/kinesthetic foundation with the six types of sensory intelligences, you may want to go back and increase the complexity of your movements. This increased neuro-motor sophistication will help you develop greater coordination, and further challenge your sensory nervous system. Every time you add a new motor complexity, the motor nervous system will try to compete for neural energy with the various sensory exercises you will be learning in the next chapters. This will force a higher level of refinement and cooperation in each sensory/motor activity you do.

## Advanced Body/Kinesthetic Exercises for Infinity Walk

### FINGER PATTERNS

As your arms swing while walking the eight pattern, touch each finger, one at a time, with your thumb on the same hand. This is more difficult than it appears, so you may want to master the finger movements before adding them to Infinity Walk. Try these patterns, or make up your own.

|  | Left Hand | Right Hand |
|---|---|---|
| Pattern I: | 1 2 3 4 | 1 2 3 4 |

In pattern I, the easiest pattern, your thumbs will simultaneously touch or tap the index fingers on each hand, then the second fingers, the third fingers and finally the little fingers, before starting the same four step sequence over again. It's easier to incorporate this finger tapping into Infinity Walk by synchronizing each tap with one arm swing. Later, a more advanced challenge is to keep the rhythm of the finger touching separate from the rhythm of your arm swings.

|  | Left Hand | Right Hand |
|---|---|---|
| Pattern II: | 1 2 3 4 | 4 3 2 1 |

After pattern I becomes easy, reverse the direction on one hand only, so your thumb on one hand is touching in ascending order, while the thumb on the second hand is touching in descending order, as shown in Pattern II. It will be easier to alternate tapping fingers between hands than to tap fingers on both hands simultaneously. If you need to, work up to keeping these two different patterns going simultaneously while you are doing Infinity Walk with full arm swings.

|  | Left Hand | Right Hand |
|---|---|---|
| Pattern III: | 1 3 2 4 | 4 2 3 1 |

Pattern III can be especially challenging to people who sometimes confuse directions or reverse letters or numbers. To prevent frustration, don't try it until you have mastered the first two! Remember, the arms must keep swinging. As you become more advanced you should be able to complete a full finger pattern in less time than it takes for your arms to swing in one direction.

139

### SHOULDER WALKS

To release tight or stiff shoulders and help your arms swing more naturally, try the following while doing Infinity Walk.

1.  Place your hands on your hips and keep them there as you do this walk. Instead of alternating swinging arms as you walk, alternate shoulders by moving each shoulder forward as the opposite leg steps forward.

2.  Raise your arms over your head and alternate each arm, stretching for the sky as the opposite leg steps forward.

3.  Alternate (1) and (2), creating a four-step sequence while doing Infinity Walk. This will take concentration.

### THE SIX STEP DANCE

If you have trouble with sense of direction, try the Six Step Dance.[6] Notice that the dance movements require you to touch your hand to your knee, thigh, or foot, from the front, side, or back of you. Continue to repeat these six steps over and over until all directions of movement come naturally to you.

To have some real fun, listen to music that has various rhythms, and keep pace with the beat of the music by tapping your knee, thigh, or foot on each of the six dance steps. This exercise is wonderful for developing rhythm, coordination, and spontaneous motor responses needed for sports, dance, and social interaction. It's also great to do when you don't have the physical space to do Infinity Walk.

### WALKING BACKWARDS

Try doing Infinity Walk in reverse. At first, you may need to look over your shoulder to see where you are walking. As you feel more confident in walking backwards, try to feel your way around the eight pattern, instead of having to rely on your vision. Remember, *your arms still need to swing with the opposite leg.* (Clue: Your arms' "forward" swing will be behind your body.) Once this is comfortable, alternate between walking one eight pattern forward, then one in reverse. Eventually, add your finger patterns to your reversed walking — for some real fun!

---

[6] I did not create this six step sequence myself but I don't have a name to give credit to. I came across it many years ago in an exercise class, and I remembered how few of the women where able to follow this sequence while keeping beat with the music.

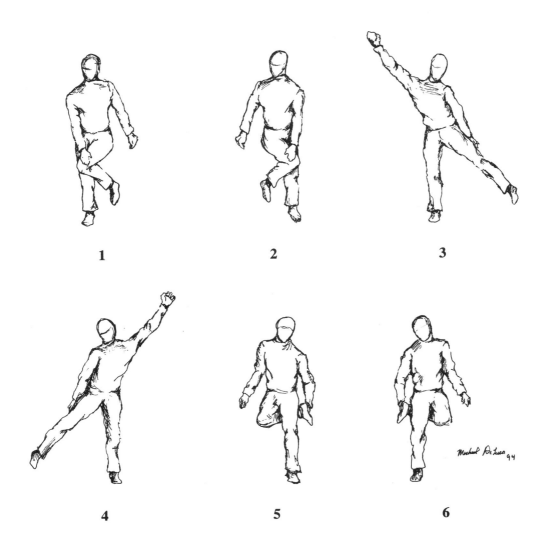

**Six Step Dance**

### WALKING FORWARD BUT REVERSING THE DIRECTION OF INFINITY WALK

Start by doing your normal Infinity Walk while looking at an object (explained in visual/spatial intelligence section on page 143). Now stop, turn around in your tracks and retrace your steps around the eight pattern, continuing to look at the same object. You'll notice that there are now two points on the eight pattern during which the object goes out of view, as your walk curves away from it. This forces you to break your eye contact and turn your head in the opposite direction to re-focus on the object. This is an excellent advanced exercise for people who are overly visually dominant, as well as for those who tend to not keep their eyes focused on the object. This advanced motor pattern requires increased balance. At first, turn your head slowly when you re-focus on the object from over your opposite shoulder, so you don't get dizzy.

### THE FOUR LEAF CLOVER

If you have enough space, you can turn Infinity Walk into a Four Leaf Clover pattern by walking two eights at 90 degree angles from each other. Walk your regular eight pattern one full time, then continue walking to the center point of the eight. From there, start the "third leaf" by walking off at a 90 degree angle, and continue until you have finished another eight pattern. Continue walking eights at these two different angles without pausing in the middle. Keep your eyes focused on the center point of the clover. This will exercise your eyes in all directions. The trick to this advanced pattern is to walk each leaf of the clover before repeating any. More concentration and short-term memory is required.

CHAPTER 11

# Adding Sensory Challenges to Infinity Walk's Motor Foundation

After observing yourself and other people doing the basic Infinity Walk pattern under various situations, you'll begin to notice how various forms of sensory, cognitive, and emotional input can throw off the motor coordination in the walk. Some people will not be able to hold a visual focus on a selected object while walking the pattern. Others will not be able to talk, or attend to auditory input without losing quality in the flow of their movements. Some may be able to attend visually or auditorily while walking clockwise but not counterclockwise. For others, the opposite will be true. The sensory skills which break down while doing the basic Infinity Walk motor pattern are, of course, the ones needing to be developed the most. If your interest is in developing just a particular type of intelligence, then go directly to that section in this chapter. However, if you have the time, I highly recommend going through this sensorimotor program one step at a time, in the order they are presented. The order of this sequence of exercises is most supportive of developing your brain's potential.

## VISUAL/SPATIAL SKILLS

3-D Visual Imaging
3-D Spatial Perception

More Right Hemisphere
Alpha

Visual/Spatial skills involve the sense of vision in our three-dimensional world. People who are naturally talented in this ability tend to be attracted to careers in art, architecture, engineering design, graphic design, construction, interior decorating, carpet installation, and landscaping. The ability to make mental images, hold them in your mind, and move them around in space is necessary to master this skill. Success at the game of chess and using maps to take a trip is dependent on this ability. In addition, three-dimensional visual/spatial abilities *must* be well developed before we can expect our visual imagination to hold images of the two-dimensional symbols of language.

The following exercises are excellent for developing visual/spatial skills and should be done *while* doing Infinity Walk.

## *Step 1. Three-Dimensional Visual Attention Span*

*Infinity Walk Point of Sensory Focus*

Look over the above drawing. Notice the location of the television in reference to the young man doing Infinity Walk. This location is called the point of sensory focus. Also notice that one of the circles of the eight pattern is walked clockwise, and the other is walked counterclockwise. Tracing the eight pattern in the diagram with your finger might help your body to feel how the direction of your walk is constantly changing from walking a circle to the right, to walking a circle to the left.

Notice how the young man's primary eye (and ear) for attending to the point of sensory focus changes as he does Infinity Walk. Depending on where he is on the eight pattern, either his left or right eye will have more responsibility for taking in the information from the television. There will also be a few moments on each circle where the young man's head is directly facing the point of sensory focus; at these times the two eyes will be at their peak potential for maximum cooperation. Moments later, as the young man takes a few more steps, the ability to face the television directly, even with his neck turned, is lost. The brain dominance for vision is forced to switch again. This sequence of right dominance, equal dominance, left dominance, equal dominance, will continue to repeat itself while walking the eight pattern and looking at the point of sensory focus.

### PRACTICE IDEAS FOR STEP 1.

Use the location of the television in the diagram as a point of reference for placing objects you wish to view while doing Infinity Walk. The smaller the object, the more challenging it will be to hold your visual attention.

Ideas for objects:
                                        television (with no sound)
candle
photo
window
written notes on poster

Vary Your Visual Distance While Doing Infinity Walk:

Focus on an object:
                                      a few feet away
across the room
at a distance (you may need to go outside if you don't have a large window)

Vary Your Visual Height While Doing Infinity Walk:

Focus on an object:
                                        on the floor
a few feet off the floor
at eye level
a few feet above eye level
on the ceiling

Now mix your possible points of visual focus, using the concepts of height and distance. For example, looking out at a far distance while looking either up or down, or looking a few feet away from you, either on the floor or at eye level. *Try to hold eye*

*contact on the object you have chosen to look at no matter what happens to the quality of your walking.* Slow down your walk if necessary, or go back to touching your upper thigh with your opposite hand as you walk. Some of these combinations of height and distance will be more difficult than others. Some may even make you dizzy at first. This is just a sign of neurological confusion, brought about by lack of experience with the particular tasks. Make a list of which ones need additional practice, so you can concentrate on them in the future.

If you are having trouble keeping your eyes focused on one point as you walk through the eight pattern, practice in front of a television, WITH THE SOUND TURNED OFF. Without sound to help you keep track of the television program, your eyes will begin to take more responsibility for holding the image. Pretend someone is going to ask you to explain the program you have just watched. This will help sharpen your visual attention span.

## Step 2. Three-Dimensional Visualization

An inability to visualize is at the root of many memory retrieval problems. Being able to visualize a situation also helps us to organize our thoughts. The better we can visualize, the more complex problem-solving we can master. Exceptional chess players, architects, scientists, artists, fiction writers, and mathematical geniuses have a highly developed ability to hold visual information long enough to be able to move the parts of the information around in their visual imaginations without losing the overall picture. They are able to image their ideas so powerfully that their visualization becomes stable, allowing them to manipulate images as if they were real objects.

If we are very auditory then we could practice combining inner hearing with inner vision. For instance, we could imagine a known voice or common sound and then look for who or what created that sound in our inner vision.

If we are very kinesthetic we could visually imagine touching and interacting with the person, place, or thing that we are trying to see internally. The richer we can make the experience, the more it will come alive.

Developing inner vision is not at odds with respecting students with auditory or kinesthetic learning styles. Students should be allowed to learn and demonstrate learnings through their preferred learning style. Let their visual practice with Infinity Walk develop outside of performance and evaluation situations.

Sometimes people who wear glasses have their inner vision trained to believe that everything should be fuzzy and unclear in their inner vision because it is in their outer vision. If this is the case, ask them to see their inner image with their glasses on, or observe it up close so they would be able to see it without glasses.

Try some of these three-dimensional visual exercises to sharpen your visual/spatial skills, and your capacity to put visual information into action. (Remember to keep your arms swinging and don't let your eight pattern get sloppy.) Visualizing while doing Infinity Walk will sharpen your ability to visually think, recall, and be creative spontaneously ("on your feet"). You'll know instantly when a particular type of visual ability needs more practice because something in either your walk or your thought process will "short circuit."

### Practice Ideas for Step 2.

### Visual Recall of Familiar Objects

While doing Infinity Walk, imagine yourself in each room of your home. Name 25 objects in each room, without losing your arm swing. See each object you name before going on to the next one. At first the objects may be fuzzy, or you may only be able to see them for a moment. Practice will improve this, allowing you to see the objects more clearly and to hold the image for longer periods of time. When this exercise becomes too easy for you, increase the challenge by keeping your eyes on a point of sensory focus during the entire exercise.

### Action Memories of Familiar People

While doing Infinity Walk create visual flashes of people you know. At first, it may be easier to rely on a specific memory to help create the image. With practice you will be able to hold the image longer. As your visual abilities improve, add motion to your images. Start with small movements like a smile, and work up to larger movements like watching the person walk, talk, or perform a familiar task. When this exercise  becomes too easy for you, increase the challenge by keeping your eyes on a point of sensory focus during the entire exercise.

### Looking For Details

While doing Infinity Walk, describe how each of your family members looks similar and different from one another. Go back as many generations as you can. See their facial features and expressions, body posture, hands, feet, etc., in detail. When you are ready, increase the challenge by keeping your eyes on a point of sensory focus during the entire exercise.

### Spatial Abilities: Getting from Here to There

While doing Infinity Walk, pick a destination at least ten miles away from your home. Visualize how you would drive there, and describe the route you would take, including all the landmarks you can visualize along the way. Say your directions out loud, as if you are giving directions to a stranger from out of town. Practice this with a number of destinations until this visual exercise becomes easy. Increase the challenge by keeping your eyes on a point of sensory focus during the entire exercise.

### Developing Creative Imagination

The Infinity Walk is a perfect foundation for the numerous creative imaging programs available today. Books such as *Mind Sight: Learning Through Imaging* and *The Mind Fitness Program for Esteem and Excellence* are dedicated to imagery exercises.[1] Any creative imagery you do can be improved by adding it to Infinity Walk. Here are some practice ideas.

1.  Organize your day by seeing yourself doing each task in the order you wish to accomplish it.

2.  Motivate yourself to start and complete a task by seeing yourself go through the details of each step of the task, including how to successfully encourage yourself to begin, and feeling accomplished when the task is completed. Go through the entire sequence of this imagery over and over again while doing Infinity Walk until you feel the urge to start the project. Then stop the walk and use this feeling to get the project started immediately. Repeat as needed.

3.  When you need a break from your daily routine take yourself on an instant vacation by imaging your idea of the perfect holiday experience. The more sensory details you add, the more you'll enjoy this exercise and feel refreshed by it.

# VERBAL/LINGUISTIC SKILLS

| | |
|---|---|
| Consistent 2-D Recognition | More Left Hemisphere |
| Attention Span for 2-D World | Beta |

---

[1] Galyean, Beverly-Colleene. *Mind Sight: Learning Through Imaging.* Berkeley, CA: Center for Integrative Learning, 1984. Goode, Caron B. and Watson, Joy Lehni. *The Mind Fitness Program for Esteem and Excellence.* Tucson, Arizona: Zephyr Press, 1992.

Verbal/linguistic skills require the ability to communicate through two-dimensional vocal and written symbols which have no meaning outside of the ones given them through group or societal consensus. These skills involve the senses of vision and/or hearing, sometimes integrated with the motor coordination of speech or hands. Therefore, even though it is a highly complex skill, most people can enjoy some competence in two-dimensional communication without complete sensorimotor integration.

People who are naturally talented in verbal/linguistic skills include salespeople, teachers, ministers, journalists, secretaries, comedians, politicians, and poets. Large gaps in verbal/linguistic abilities can be found in these fields as well. A poet may have difficulty spelling. A minister may give inspiring spontaneous sermons but have writer's block. A secretary may excel in correcting someone else's spelling and grammar but feel unable to write creatively. A journalist may be excellent at writing up a story but poor at interviewing the people involved. The following exercises can expand and refine verbal/linguistic skills and help put them into action.

## Step 1.  Two-Dimensional Visual Attention Span

Before we can expect to excel in two-dimensional language we must develop a good attention span for holding these symbols in our minds. The following exercises will sharpen your abilities in this important skill. It's important to note that many creative people have not mastered written language because the two-dimensional realm does not hold their interest. Therefore, try to make these exercises especially fun.

### PRACTICE IDEAS FOR STEP 1.

### Visual Memory, Counting, and Sequencing

While doing Infinity Walk, count and describe every detail of everything you have done today, in the order you have done them. Mentally see yourself going through your experiences of the day. Count each experience by saying the number out loud, and  continue this exercise until you have remembered and visualized 50 details about your day. When this exercise becomes too easy for you, increase the challenge by keeping your eyes on a point of sensory focus, and by snapping your fingers each time you say a number out loud. Do this without losing the rhythm of your arm swings.

### Visual Alternation of Numbers and Letters

While doing Infinity Walk, alternate between counting the numbers 1-26 with reciting the alphabet, i.e., 1 a 2 b 3 c 4 d 5 e . . .   etc. After you can do this with ease, practice reciting it backwards, i.e., 26 z 25 y 24 x 23 w .  . . . This will not be easy to do unless you can focus your inner vision to see every letter and number. If you learned the alphabet by sound in early grade school, you will have the added challenge of learning it for the first time by visual recognition and memory.

### *More Practice with Holding Numbers as Objects in Your Mind*

While doing Infinity Walk see the following numbers in your mind. It may help to imagine yourself writing them down or keying them into a computer.

Count forward by 3's, up to 99, i.e., 3, 6, 9, . . .

Count forward by 4's up to 100, i.e., 4, 8, 12, . . .

Count backwards by 3's, i.e., 99, 96, 93, . . .

Count backwards by 4's, i.e., 100, 96, 92, . . .

When this exercise becomes too easy for you, increase the challenge by keeping your eyes on a point of sensory focus, and by snapping your fingers — on your forward swinging hand only — each time you say a number out loud. Do this without losing the rhythm of your arm swings.

### *Visual Attention Span for Letters: Holding Words in Your Mind*

Image a word you know how to spell. You may need to see yourself write or type it to hold it steady. Play with the letters by changing their size, color, and shifting between caps and lower case typeset, and your own printing and script. After you have developed some competence for manipulating the individual letters, spell the word in reverse by looking at each letter from right to left. You can visualize erasing the letters one at a time, or pretend you are hitting the backspace key on a typewriter or computer keyboard and watching each letter disappear. This exercise can't be over-practiced. It is essential to developing photographic memory and mastering spelling and word recognition. When this exercise becomes too easy for you, increase the challenge by keeping your eyes on a point of sensory focus during the entire exercise.

## *Step 2. Photographic Memory and Spelling*

English is not one of the easier languages to master; any foreigner can tell you that. One of the reasons we have a difficult language is because we cannot count on phonetics (the sound of words) to help us spell or recognize the meanings of many written words.[2]

The medical field has wisely stayed with Latin in its constant creation of new terminology. Each syllable has a specific meaning, is easy to phonetically pronounce because each letter or combination of letters has only one possible sound assigned to it, and syllables can be used in combinations to create new but related meanings. New words can be introduced easily without having people visually memorize a whole new spelling or auditorily memorize a foreign sequence of sounds. Some of the prefixes and suffixes that change the root meanings of English words are examples of Latin influence on our language.

The spelling of English words is best mastered through the visual sense. I can use my own childhood experience here to help illustrate this point. I was primarily an auditory learner in grade school. I depended a great deal on sound recognition to create order out of language. I learned the alphabet by singing it, and received sufficient praise to believe this was how one should memorize language. However, I never had a picture of the letters in my visual imagination as I sang, so I learned only the sequence of sounds, not the sequence of written letters. This oversight reached the height of a frustrating quirk in my intelligence when, in college, I would constantly find myself humming pieces of the alphabet song just to find my way around the card index file in the library!

I used to memorize important telephone numbers the same way, by creating a sing-song melody for each phone number. Unfortunately, if I forgot a melody, the phone number would be unretrievable. I've been told by musicians that I have near perfect pitch when singing without a musical accompaniment. If they only knew! Survival skills are often practiced to perfection.

Photographic memory is the direct visual equivalent of perfect pitch. Both could be natural, common abilities available to all of us if only we allowed ourselves to experience life more fully, through more than one mode of perception at a time. In fact, the method I am going to suggest here is not just for spelling, but will enhance everyone's photographic memory.

Everyone I have worked with who had difficulty spelling either (1) had not developed their natural abilities to see and hold clear pictures in their visual imaginations; (2) had never taken the time to see the details of every letter of the

---

[2] Phonics is a very important first step for learning to recognize the relationship between written symbols and sounds. This book does not cover the topic, but your library can help you find good books on the topic if you are just starting to help someone learn to read.

two-dimensional words clearly in their visual imaginations, even though they might have had an excellent capacity to visualize three-dimensional images; or (3) their choice of the location in their heads to visualize words was not the best for quick and accurate visual memory retrieval.

First, we must have a capacity to visualize pictures either inside our heads or projected out in front of our heads. If we can't visualize two-dimensional letters and numbers, then we need to start with three-dimensional images (visual/spatial) that are familiar to us: our own homes, our cars, a favorite pet, faces of people we know well. Picturing people, places, and things that have an emotional impact (theta brain waves) can make the images clearer. It is not necessary for each image to be held more than a second or two at first. More important are the images' clarity and the amount of detail that is available. As long as our inner vision gets even a moment to view a clear, detailed image, we will have whatever information we were looking for in a retrievable form. The visual/spatial section, starting on page 143 of this chapter, can help develop this three-dimensional ability.

Second, we must be able to accurately hold two-dimensional symbols in our minds. Some people need help at first to create the visual details of words — the letters. To make sure they are really taking the time to create an accurately spelled word in their visual memory I'll ask them questions about the word they see in their mind. How many letters can they count in the word? Does this word have a color? Are all the letters the same color and size? Are there any "i's" or "l's" in this word? How many? These questions allow the person to analyze the word as if it were written on a chalkboard in a classroom. The exercises for two-dimensional attention span, which start on page 149, can help develop this two-dimensional ability.

The exercises in this section are for the third cause of spelling difficulty — the place people are looking inside their heads to see words is not the best for quick and accurate visual memory retrieval. The movement of eye muscles triggers different parts of our brain. For instance, looking far right gives dominance to the left brain and language center (for 95% of all people), and looking in an upward direction can help us visualize.

With a little experimenting, you can help someone find their own best place to see words clearly and correctly. Ask them to see their name in their head where they usually visualize words. Then suggest they try other places, including over their right and left eyebrow. The place they see their name clearest and can hold the image longest is usually the best spot for correct spelling input and retrieval. When I find people totally stuck, with no word imaging ability at all, I will guide them by suggesting that they try looking up and to the right inside their head or over their eyebrow. Of course, no one but the owner of the brain can tell us how it works best. I've had people whose spelling improved after finding their best visual spot to be on the left side of their foreheads. I've also known children who had a well developed visual ability on their left side but it handicapped them on written spelling tests because they were right-handed. Checking their sensorimotor pattern, using the method in chapter 8, can sometimes help you understand unusual responses. For instance, if the person has a mixed eye-ear dominance, looking toward the dominant ear won't help develop visual spelling abilities. If the person has a mixed eye-hand dominance, you will need to experiment a little more to decide which side gives more retrievable written information.

There does seem to be some loss of communication, for some people, between left and right sides of the brain when switching from vision or hearing on one side to writing on the other. I used to have this problem on the phone with my dominant left ear and right hand. Trying to copy down phone numbers over the phone was humorous, to say the least. I would be completely sure I was writing the number down exactly as it was being given to me, just to find out, over and over, that it was incorrect. This quirk was corrected instantly by adding a middle step that takes only a fraction of a second. Now, I hear the numbers in my left ear, see them over my right eyebrow, and then send them down the same side of my body into my right hand. This eliminates all of those mysterious errors.

Those of you who have studied neurolinguistic programming (NLP), which assesses the relationship between eye positions and inner processing, will need to be especially careful to not decide for someone what they are really doing as they move their eyes to retrieve a spelling word. For example, looking down may indicate a kinesthetic or bodily sensing that moves away from visual imaging. However, like most rules, this holds true only sometimes.

I have been able to help some very frustrated adults with spelling by noticing that every time they looked down, their visual minds would go blank; and for some unknown reason, they would look down each time they tried to recall the spelling of a word. However, there have been other times that I could have been fooled by this tendency. I always start a spelling session by having students discover for themselves where to look in their heads to find a word. Some of them have actually been most successful when looking down. These students have told me that they were visualizing up around their forehead while they looked down. This looking down for them was more a way to create privacy. I often do this myself while I am visualizing. In fact, I find it a comfortable eye position for accessing all modes of sensory input simultaneously, because it does not bias any one particular mode.

Some people who reverse letters or leave out a letter or two are spelling their words across the middle of their foreheads instead of to the left or right of center. I think that inner vision works very much the same way as outer vision. That is, left and right inner visual images are more easily accessed by the opposite hemispheres. Anything in the middle risks the possibility that the two hemispheres will fight over dominating the image, and letters can be lost, reversed, or placed out of order in the process. This can be solved by making sure no letters in a word are being spelled across the middle of the forehead.

This became obvious to me after working with a number of otherwise bright children who were having trouble with spelling. Eventually, I could tell them where on their foreheads they were seeing a word by which part of the word they tended to consistently leave out or misspell. If you have a child or student who consistently errs in the beginning, middle, or end of a word, you can be sure they have a placement problem.

One common cause of this problem is that some children draw the letters too large in their minds, so that they don't all fit on one side. Simply asking them to make the letters smaller solves this problem.

### PRACTICE IDEAS FOR STEP 2.

### Seeing Familiar Words Internally

While doing Infinity Walk practice seeing words over your right or left eyebrow, whichever works better for you. It's not necessary to see internally if images can be "seen" externally. Some people have had success learning to imagine words written on their forearm or hand. Try the following. Think of three-letter words and see their individual letters forward and then *backwards (right to left)*. Increase the length of the words up to seven letters. As you improve, increase your challenge by holding your eyes on a point of sensory focus while your inner vision continues to clearly and correctly view words over the preferred eyebrow.

### *Learning New Spelling Words*

Collect words you frequently misspell and write them on something easily seen while doing Infinity Walk. Write each word so it is divided up by syllables (e.g. syl la bles). Your dictionary can help if you are not sure how to divide a word up into single uninterrupted sounds. Place these written words at your point of sensory focus.

As you do Infinity Walk see each word one syllable at a time over your preferred eyebrow. Take the time to look carefully at each letter in the syllable unit before going on to the next syllable. When you feel confident you have developed photographic memory for the word, look away from your written notes and see and "read" the letters from your internal visual image. If you are experiencing true photographic memory you will also be able to read the word backwards, from right to left. Be sure to maintain a good figure eight pattern and arm swing throughout this exercise.

### *Creating Proper Diction*

While doing Infinity Walk use the spelling exercise to create proper diction. Each syllable is a separate distinct sound controlled by the consonants and vowels in it. Every spoken syllable forces the organs of speech to reshape themselves. Thus you can actually feel a repositioning of your lips, tongue, jaw, throat, and cheek muscles as you move from one syllable to the next. While doing Infinity Walk talk out loud very slowly and exaggerate the repositioning of your speech muscles as you see each syllable over your preferred eyebrow. Pay attention to the consonants and vowels you are seeing in your inner vision and shape your syllable sounds around what you see, rather than your habitual way of speaking. This exercise also improves spelling because it helps us notice that how we pronounce a word can confuse how we spell it. It also identifies words that cannot be correctly spelled by phonics alone, alerting our photographic inner vision to pay special attention to the correct visual image of the word.

## MUSICAL/RHYTHMIC SKILLS

| Inner Timing | Mostly Right Hemisphere |
| --- | --- |
| Mood and Motivation | Beta, Alpha, and Theta |

Musical/Rhythmic Skills add quality to our inner life experience and proper timing to our outer life performance. Our entire biological process runs on a life rhythm. Brain waves, heart rate, and respiration have a range of rhythms that span high anxiety to deep tranquillity. So it should be no surprise that researchers have discovered that music and rhythmic patterns have a profound influence on our biological rhythms.[3] Music can change a person's mood faster than any other sensory input. A strong musical rhythm can shift our bio-rhythms, causing shifts in motivation. There's nothing like good rock and roll for speed cleaning a house, or soft, slow classical music for unwinding at the end of a long day. Skill at shifting internal rhythms through sound is so valuable that Howard Gardner recognized it as a separate form of intelligence.[4]

People who are naturally talented in musical/rhythmic skills often find their way into fields involving music. They may teach, perform, or compose. However, if the kinesthetic body or motor coordination isn't well integrated with a person's musical/rhythmic skills, they will be limited to only appreciating the mood altering sounds. The joy of creating music or moving the body to the rhythm of music may never be realized. Music appreciation requires mainly the right hemisphere and the lower brain limbic system. Music composition also requires the left hemisphere's organizational skills in the beta range.

## Step 1. Balanced Listening

Place a speaker at the point of sensory focus. This is the only location that will properly exercise your auditory sensory system while doing the Infinity Walk. If you are working with a stereo system, adjust the sound so that it is coming from only the speaker at the point of sensory focus. Try the following ideas while doing Infinity Walk. *Look at the speaker at all times, and imagine the corresponding (same-sided) ear intentionally listening to the auditory output from the speaker.*

PRACTICE IDEAS FOR STEP 1.

Listen to:

　　Talk shows on the radio

　　Audiotaped lectures, talking books, or study notes

　　Television with sound on, but screen covered

---

[3] Campbell, D. *Introduction to the Musical Brain.* Saint Louis, Missouri: MMB Music, 1986. Halpern, Steven. *Tuning the Human Instrument.* Belmont, CA: Spectrum Research Institute, 1978.

[4] Gardner, H. *Frames of Mind: The Theory of Multiple Intelligences.* New York: Harper and Row, 1983.

## Step 2. *Integrating Auditory and Visual Input*

*The value of strengthening your ability to use your vision and hearing in a coordinated and cooperative way is infinite.* For people who have a mixed eye and ear dominance, as discussed in Chapter 8, the development of visual/auditory cooperation is essential. When we do Infinity Walk with the use of a visual and auditory stimulus aid, as seen in the above diagram, we are also teaching the eye and ear on the same side of the head to cooperate. This helps alleviate the potential handicaps of mixed visual/auditory dominance.

### PRACTICE IDEAS FOR STEP 2.

When you feel confident that the quality of your Infinity Walk is not sacrificed by either visual or auditory input you can combine the two sensory modes while walking. Those of you who enjoy television can now enjoy viewing with the sound. This can be a great incentive for children, too. Those of you who wish to use Infinity Walk for study purposes may combine written study notes taped on the wall or placed on a table opposite the center of your eight pattern (point of sensory focus), with audiotaped study notes covering the same material. The combination of seeing and hearing the study materials we wish to master, while doing the Infinity Walk, greatly increases our ability to naturally absorb information through both senses and across both hemispheres. Information absorbed this way will be more readily retrievable through our motor system at a later point, regardless of your present eye-ear-hand dominance pattern.

## Step 3. *Developing Your Voice*

Try some of the following exercises while doing Infinity Walk to develop and strengthen the neural communication between sensory input of your voice through your ears and motor output through your speech muscles. Throughout the exercise listen as carefully to your voice as you would to another person's.

### PRACTICE IDEAS FOR STEP 3.

Hum along with a musical recording; try music that has lyrics as well as instrumental music.

Listen to a musical recording of an orchestra, and use your voice to mimic the sounds of the various instruments.

Sing along with popular vocal tunes.

Memorize words to a song by playing the recording a number of times; then sing the song without the music.

### Learning to Carry a Tune

If you have trouble carrying a tune when you sing, pick a very simple nursery rhyme, or repeat a short, well known song over and over as you walk. Listen to the sound of your voice and play with the sound instead of being concerned about getting it right. Make your voice sound different each time you sing it. Imagine playing your voice the way a talented musician can play an instrument. There are an infinite number of sounds and emotions you can create with your voice while singing the words to a simple little nursery rhyme. Focus on walking with the rhythm of the tune, and start to feel the song turning into a dance in your body. Express the song through your body first; your voice will follow. Some ideas for songs: "Mary had a Little Lamb," "Row, Row, Row Your Boat," "London Bridge is Falling Down," "Old MacDonald had a Farm," "Happy Birthday." Nursery rhymes are also great for bringing out your alpha/theta child hidden away inside you. Imagine you are splashing through puddles of rainwater as you walk the eight pattern and sing your nursery rhyme! Singing songs from early childhood can help unlock your dormant playfulness and spontaneity.

## Step 4. Music for Mood and Motivation

Select a variety of music to listen to while doing Infinity Walk. Each musical piece should produce a specific, identifiable mood in you. Set up a stereo speaker so it is positioned (only) at the point of sensory focus. You can also place an object for visual focus by the speaker if you like. As you do Infinity Walk, the music and rhythms you have chosen will flow into your left and right ears, sending the vibrations deep into both hemispheres as well as the lower brain limbic system that controls emotion and motivation. The rhythmic vibrations are also felt by the surface of your entire body.

### PRACTICE IDEAS FOR STEP 4.

### Adjusting Your Attitude

Collect music that creates the following effects in you. Label the music by the effect it creates and keep it available for doing the Infinity Walk on a moment's notice when you need an "attitude adjustment." Your body should move with the rhythm of the music, so the speed of your walk and the power of your arm swings will shift with your selection.

Your music collection should include favorites that:

1.  calm tension or anxiety
2.  relieve fatigue
3.  put a smile on your face
4.  stimulate desire to move your body faster
5.  increase feelings of self-worth
6.  create tender feelings of love
7.  inspire humanitarian ideals
8.  focus your thoughts and goals
9.  release pent up emotions

### Balancing the Rhythm of Breath

Choose a slow, relaxing piece of music with a steady rhythm for this exercise. As you do Infinity Walk and listen to your musical selection, alternate yawning on the inhale with sighing on the exhale of each breath. Every yawn should be a slow opened mouthed authentic yawn, fully enjoyed and savored. The sighed exhale should begin the moment you stop inhaling, so there is no time in which you are holding your breath. Keep it slow and rhythmic. It you begin to get dizzy you may be breathing too fast, so slow it down even more. This exercise brings a feeling of deep relaxation and inner peace, and can improve your normal rhythm of breathing with practice.

## Step 5. Musical Training

Infinity Walk has proven useful to a number of musicians. I've had music teachers report that students perform their instrumental lessons better after doing Infinity Walk for a few minutes at the beginning of a lesson. One piano teacher said she has her students use the piano as the point of sensory focus and has them hear the musical piece in their minds while their eyes look toward the sheet music on the piano. Another uses the Infinity Walk to help clear and focus the students' minds, and activate both sides of the body for two-handed playing. Both say the lessons go much better. The students are more alert and their playing sounds "more practiced."

I've also had students I've worked with pretend they are playing their musical instrument while doing Infinity Walk. With arms fully swinging they do the finger positions for musical scales. This is a very advanced form of the finger pattern exercises presented on page 139. It requires a great deal of sensorimotor integration, but is a highly motivating challenge to the gifted student interested in accelerated learning. Students who have imagined practicing their instruments while doing Infinity Walk have reported excellent progress when actually playing the instrument later.

## Step 6. Adding Other Sources to Infinity Walk

There's a wealth of information on the market about the relationship between music and learning[5] and music's ability to alter brain wave frequencies and mood.[6] All of these methods can be added to Infinity Walk to incorporate the dimensions of music, mood, and rhythm into the motor nervous system and action. Whether you are interested in improving artistic performance, looking for a better relationship with your emotions, or just interested in enjoying the pleasures of sound and movement more, combining these programs with Infinity Walk will help you succeed in your goal.

# INTERPERSONAL SKILLS

Effective Communication
Motor Nerves of Speech Muscles

Both Hemispheres
Beta and Alpha, with strong auditory

Interpersonal skills include effective verbal and non-verbal communication. These skills are needed to be sensitive to others' needs and feelings, to work cooperatively with others, and to discern others' underlying motivations and intentions.[7] Team cooperation is necessary for couples, families, organizations, institutions, and any situation where two or more people are needed to accomplish a goal. These social skills can be learned behaviorally or can be a natural reflection of an intuitive, empathic personality. In the latter case, theta feelings may be present, as well as beta language and organization and alpha problem-solving. A lack of interpersonal skills can be a severe handicap regardless of having other types of intelligences and resources. Without it, people are likely to receive little emotional or social support for their personal endeavors. In fact, society tends to punish people who are unskilled in interpersonal communication by ostracizing them.

---

[5] Brewer, Chris, and Campbell, Don. *Rhythms of Learning: Creative Tools for Developing Lifelong Skills.* Tucson, Arizona: Zephyr Press, 1991. Campbell, Don. *100 Ways to Improve Teaching Using Your Voice and Music: Pathways to Accelerate Learning.* Tucson, Arizona: Zephyr Press, 1992. Webb, Terry Wyler, and Webb, Douglas. *Accelerated Learning with Music.* Norcross, Georgia: Accelerated Learning Systems, 1990.

[6] Houston, Jean. *The Possible Human.* Los Angeles: J.P. Tarcher, 1982. Halpern, Steven. *Tuning the Human Instrument.* Belmont, CA: Spectrum Research Institute, 1978.

[7] Lazear, David. *Seven Ways of Knowing: Understanding Multiple Intelligences.* Palatine, Illinois: Skylight Publishing, 1991.

People who are naturally talented in interpersonal skills can be successful in careers involving leadership and positions of authority. Counselors, educators, politicians, actors and stage performers, business managers, small business owners, and salespeople all require good interpersonal skills to succeed at their trade.

## Step 1. Improving Conversational Language

Our ability to speak fluidly and effectively may be improved through Infinity Walk by practicing the following exercises that involve visualization, speech, and motor action:

### PRACTICE IDEAS FOR STEP 1.

### Level I. Talking Out Loud to Yourself without Audience

You have already begun your practice of the first step to fluid speech. As you described various memories and past experiences out loud in the section on verbal/linguistic skills, you were using your speaking voice. However, there is a difference between talking to review information for our own benefit and speaking with comfort and confidence to another person. In this section, we will practice some of the preceding exercises again, only this time with more focus on your presentation style. As you do Infinity Walk, pretend someone is sitting and listening to you speak. Place this imaginary person at the point of sensory focus. At first choose people with whom you are already comfortable speaking. Then, increase the potential stress in the situation by imaging people with whom you would feel less confident.

### Neutral Situations with Imaginary Audience:

While doing Infinity Walk, speak to the following imaginary people out loud; be sure to keep your eyes focused on "them."

1. Give directions to a stranger on how to drive across the city.
2. Tell a friend everything you have done today.
3. Share a happy childhood memory with a family member.

### Emotionally Charged Situations with Imaginary Audience:

1. While doing Infinity Walk, orally review your study notes by pretending your teacher or professor is sitting in front of you and quizzing you.
2. While doing Infinity Walk, interview for a new job with an unfriendly interviewer. Convince the interviewer that you are perfect for the job.

3. While doing Infinity Walk, tell a friend or family member something about him or her that has been bothering you. Be constructive in your feedback, but make it clear that you don't appreciate their behavior.

4. While doing Infinity Walk, tell your mother, father, sister, or brother (whomever it is more difficult for you to talk with) how much you care about him or her, or how much you wish you could be closer to him or her, if you don't feel close now.

## Level II. Talking to a Real Audience

Now find opportunities to talk with family, friends, co-workers, neighbors, etc., while doing Infinity Walk. If you are studying for an exam, ask someone to listen to you speak on the topic you are reviewing. Family members can take turns doing Infinity Walk while sharing their day with each other. Remember to maintain eye contact with the person sitting at the point of sensory focus. (Take this opportunity of having someone present to also get feedback on your body/kinesthetic skills while doing Infinity Walk.)

## Level III. Conversing with a Real Audience

Most difficult of all can be spontaneous conversation, where you never know what another person might say or ask. If you sometimes feel stuck for words when someone catches you off guard, this can be a good exercise for you.

### Neutral Situations:

1. Carry on a natural conversation with a friend or family member, each taking turns to talk.

2. Discuss plans for a vacation, day trip, or evening out.

### Emotionally Charged Situations:

1. Have your friend test you on materials you are studying. This person should question you on your answers and ask for clarity or more information, as needed. Afterwards, ask for constructive feedback.

2. Have a friend pretend to interview you for a job. Ask them to not make it too easy for you. Afterwards, ask for constructive feedback.

3. Tell the person who is your audience everything you like about them, and why. Then, with their permission, give them constructive feedback on something you believe they would appreciate but may find difficult to hear. Be positive but clear. Continue to walk, swinging your arms and making eye contact, as the two of you discuss what has been said.

Next, ask your friend to give you constructive feedback on something that may be difficult to hear. Listen carefully while maintaining eye contact and breathe gently and rhythmically, and keep those arms swinging! Imagine your friend's perspective rather than your own while listening. Wait until your friend is finished before responding. Respond by thanking your friend first, then speak about how the information may have a positive influence on you in the future.

## Step 2. *Interpersonal Problem-Solving with Infinity Walk*

Infinity Walk is an excellent means to problem-solving interpersonal conflicts. As we walk (1) we can identify our predominant emotion; (2) review the situation that has caused this emotion to reach a level of discomfort in our bodies; (3) remind ourselves of the personal qualities and talents that we can utilize to overcome the stress in this particular situation; and (4) create a powerful statement we can use to move us through the discomfort of the emotion and channel the electrical energy of the emotion into an appropriate and productive action. These all come easier while doing Infinity Walk because "hidden" knowledge or insights can spring up into our conscious minds from this integrative exercise.

There are two practice examples below. Read through them to get an idea of how to create your own. Then do Infinity Walk, with a visual focus, as you talk through your situation out loud, using the four steps.

*PRACTICE EXAMPLES FOR STEP 2.*

*Identify Emotion:*     *Anxiety*

Situation:

I'm terrified of looking for a new job. I lose my confidence as soon as I walk into  the interview. I can never think of the right thing to say. I sound so stupid, why would someone want to hire me?

Personal Qualities:

I know I'm a lot more intelligent than I interview. In fact, once I'm comfortable in a new job, I'm an excellent employee. I'm a good worker, a real asset to the company. It's to their benefit that they hire me.

Action Statement:

I'm going to tell the interviewer all the reasons I make a good employee. I'm going to tell them that my initial shyness sometimes hides my qualities. I'm going to tell them what I'm like on the job, once I'm comfortable with the new environment. I'm going to convince them that I have much more to offer their company than they may be seeing in my interview. I am not going to let my insecurities cover up my qualities. I deserve this job, and the company will be lucky to get me, as well.

### *Identify Emotion:*     *Anger*

Situation:

I'm so angry at him that I could scream! How dare my boss treat me that way! He acts like the company hired me as his personal slave; and no matter how much effort I put into the job, it's never good enough for him.

Personal Qualities:

I'm an excellent employee because [list reasons]. I deserve every penny the company pays me. My work stands on its own; I don't need my boss's approval to tell me how valuable I am to the company.

Action Statement:

Monday morning I'm looking into a transfer to another department. My boss will just have to find someone else to abuse. If the company can't move me to a better department within a few months, I'm going to start looking for a new job in my spare time. I'm going to find a job where the employees are appreciated, and rewarded for their efforts.

Summarize your own interpersonal situations you would like to resolve. Then do Infinity Walk while going through the following steps. Let your walk feel powerful as you talk yourself through each situation.

1)  Identify the emotion you are feeling.

2)  Summarize the situation in a few sentences.

3)  Summarize your available qualities, abilities, and resources.

4)  Create an action statement to follow through on.

As you do Infinity Walk, refine your self-talk each time you go through it so the situation becomes more clear and your solution more feasible the longer you walk. Try to take some positive action, however small, toward resolving the problem the moment you stop doing Infinity Walk. You'll be surprised how much easier it is to problem-solve while doing Infinity Walk than just sitting and thinking about a problem. The more brain function you can access, the more the problem seems to solve itself. Be sure to keep your eyes focused and talk out loud.

# LOGICAL/MATHEMATICAL SKILLS

Objective Reasoning

Abstract Understanding

"Order out of Chaos"

Both Hemispheres

Beta and Alpha, Strong Visual

Logical/Mathematical skills include the cognitive manipulation of three-dimensional objects, two-dimensional symbols, language generated ideas, and abstract concepts. These skills are needed for cognitive problem-solving, finances, and pursuing new ideas and discoveries in the three-dimensional world. Logical/mathematical abilities draw on the left brain's ability to recognize and relate two-dimensional symbols to three-dimensional objects and ideas. They also draw on the right brain's ability to link a multitude of these identifiable symbols together in an almost infinite number of combinations and patterns, resulting in new information and solutions. This highly complex whole brain skill creates order out of chaos, and new solutions out of old information.

People who are naturally talented in logical/mathematical skills do well in fields of research, finance, law and medicine, administration, computer technology, music composition, orchestra conducting, and film making. Obviously, this complex skill builds on some of the earlier ones practiced through Infinity Walk.

Piaget, famous for his extensive study of children's cognitive development, concluded that the abstract reasoning possible through logical/mathematical abilities is  the highest developmental stage of *cognitive* intelligence.[8] This is not a judgment on

---

[8] Piaget, Jean. *The Psychology of Intelligence.* Totowa, NJ: Littlefield Adams, 1972. Piaget, J. and Inhelder, B. *The Language and Thought of a Child.* New York: Meridian, 1955.

being the *best* kind of intelligence, but rather an understanding that it requires the most complete and integrated cognitive cooperation of the two brain hemispheres to master. Hence I have placed it second to last in Infinity Walk's progressive exercises. Of Gardner's seven types of intelligence, only intrapersonal intelligence demands more of the whole brain's integrated cooperation at all brain wave frequencies. The following exercises can help expand and refine logical/mathematical skills and help put them into action.

## Step 1. *Creative Integration of Symbols and Hemispheres*

Turning left hemisphere beta two-dimensional symbols, whether they are words or numbers, into something meaningful in the three-dimensional world is the first step to developing logical/mathematical intelligence. The following creative exercise is also excellent for verbal/linguistic people who are comfortable with language symbols, but lose their advantage when it comes to number symbols.

In the following examples, historical dates and phone numbers are memorized through an ordered sequence of creative three-dimensional images. As you read through these descriptive stories, use your visual imagination to help make the numbers represent three-dimensional reality. Once you learn how to do this exercise it should be done while doing Infinity Walk. Try not to let your eyes look away from the point of sensory focus as you create new number images.

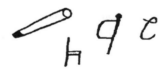

*1492 Columbus finds the new world*

See Columbus on his boat holding a telescope that looks like a number one. He spots land, and has his crew put a smaller row boat in the water so he can explore the coastline. See Columbus in the rowboat, sitting on a chair that looks like an upside down four, while the sailors row him to shore. When they reach the shore Columbus sticks a flag in the sand that looks amazingly like a number nine. Then he goes fishing with a hook that looks like the number two when it is upside down.

Can you recreate this story from the numbers 1492 ?

### 1776 Declaration of Independence

See men signing a document with a feather pen that looks like the number one. They are all standing under a protective umbrella made up of two number seven's. They need this protection because the English and England's friends are not happy about the American colonies declaring their independence from England. The men are all wearing powdered wigs with long curls. As one of the men walks away, a curl from his wig that looks like the number six gets caught on the umbrella and he almost loses his wig.

Can you recreate this story from the numbers 1776 ?

### 1903 Wright brothers make their first airplane flight

The Wright brothers are tightening the last screws on their new airplane with a screwdriver that looks like a number one. They want to make sure everything is right (Wright) before they try to fly. The plane looks like a big dragonfly as it starts to take off down the grassy field, and that dragonfly looks like a number nine on its side, with the circle in the nine representing the wings of the dragonfly and the plane. The onlooking crowds open their mouths wide with surprise when the dragonfly plane leaves the ground by a few inches, making their mouths look like big zeroes. But the plane bumps back down, and bumps along the ground across the field, making it look like a boat riding choppy waves, and that reminds me of the waves in the number three.  Finally the plane takes off.

Can you recreate this story from the numbers 1903 ?

Longer numbers like phone numbers can be memorized in the same way. Instead of relating the numbers to history, relate them to something personally meaningful about the owner of the phone number. Here's an example.

*746-8100 Local Library*

I see myself walking into my local library. I pass the book drop as I walk in. The book drop door reminds me of the number seven swinging on a hinge. Next I walk past an information desk with a hard chair. The chair looks like an upside down four. I then notice a potted plant on the desk. It has one lily of the valley blooming that looks like an upside down six to me. I take out my glasses so I can look something up in the card index file. My glasses remind me of the number eight. Then I take out my pen, that looks like a number one, to write down some information. I get the book I am looking for and sit down at a table to read. I take two small balls out of my purse and place them under my bare feet so I can massage the bottoms of my feet while I read. These two balls remind me of two zeros.

Can you recreate my trip to the library from the numbers 746-8100 ?

Here are some helpful hints for success with this method:

1. Always create the story as a sequence of events representing each number so the order of the numbers doesn't get confused. Practice recalling the story in the correct sequence only.

2. Make the stories both meaningful and interesting. You'll remember them better this way.

3. Never use the same visual image for two different numbers. Some numbers look similar, such as the two and the five; only one of them should represent, for example, a fishing hook. Both the seven and the nine could be seen as a flag, so choose only one to represent a flag. Otherwise you'll find yourself uncertain as to which number you intended to use in a story.

4. Don't be concerned about the time it might take you to create number stories at first. All the time you spend creating number stories is time spent developing

your creativity and logical/mathematical skills, as well as brushing up on visual/spatial and verbal/linguistic abilities. It's time well spent.

5.  If you have a special interest in developing this skill, pick a new number sequence to memorize weekly. Frequently used phone numbers are a good place to start. With time, you'll find your whole brain creativity improving, and the time needed to problem-solve each story sequence shortening.

## PRACTICE IDEAS FOR STEP 1.

Here's a list of possible number images to get you started:

### Number One

any stick-like object

candle

match

fence post

lamp post

tall thin tree

telephone pole

butter knife

pencil/pen

telescope

feather

ruler

fireplace poker

### Number Two

Fishing hook

Christmas ornament hook

Drapery hook

lawn chair with sun shade

reclining chair on a hinge

### *Number Three*

open clam shell
ocean waves
flying bird
bongo drums
mountain range
breasts
musical castanets (hinged 3)
lobster claws (hinged 3)
pinchers (hinged 3)
musical triangle (3 corners)

### *Number Four*

straight chair (upside down)
2 pronged fork
sign on a post

### *Number Five*

big spoon
ice cream scooper
bulldozer shovel
5 pointed star fish
stars (five pointed)

### *Number Six*

long curl of hair
rope with loop on the end
lily of the valley flower (upside down)
balloon on a string (upside down)
ear (upside down)

### *Number Seven*

arrow or pointer
playground slide
swinging hinged door

sharp pointed nose

golf club (upside down)

half an umbrella

## *Number Eight*

eyes

eye glasses

binoculars

totem pole with two heads

figure eight in ice skating, horse shows

snowman

"infinity" viewed at the horizon

## *Number Nine*

flag on a pole

hobo's bag on a stick

dragonfly

other flying insects

plane with large wings

helicopter

bubble blower

snail

musical note

## *Number Zero*

ball

wheel

ring

orange, apple (round fruit)

globe

marble

button

egg in shell

basketball hoop

open mouth

## Step 2. Art of Efficient Living

Prioritizing your time and your mental and physical energy around short and long term goals to achieve daily satisfaction while fulfilling life-long dreams requires all the skills of logical/mathematical intelligence.[9] The following exercise can be done daily or weekly, and is a great help in organizing your life to reach your dreams. In addition, the more you practice it, the more you will exercise your logical/mathematical intelligence, which will in turn increase your skill in carrying out efficient living.

PRACTICE IDEAS FOR STEP 2.

While doing Infinity Walk:

1) Prioritize your goals for the day, week, and month.

2) List your personal needs for the same time period.

3) Sort your goals and needs into one list.

4) Analyze how your list helps or hinders your dreams.

5) Refine your list until it meets your short and long term goals, responsibilities, and dreams.

6) Problem-solve your results until they seem feasible.

7) Order them so they can be scheduled with time and energy efficiency.

8) Keep paper and pen handy to write your finished thoughts down in between doing Infinity Walk.

9) Improve and update your conclusions each time you do Infinity Walk.

10) Always carry out something prioritized on your list every time you finish doing Infinity Walk for the day.

## Step 3. Improving Math Problem-Solving

With the age of calculators and computers the ability to solve mathematical problems is less practiced. Although these electronic devices are faster and more accurate than our own mental calculations, it is still valuable to exercise this skill because it helps keep our logical/mathematical intelligence sharp. Try the following mental exercises while doing Infinity Walk, then make up some of your own.

---

[9] Common sense grows out of logical intelligence. Next time you hear students complain of having to study math, a sucject they "will never use," you can explain this to them.

PRACTICE IDEAS FOR STEP 3.

1) Solve addition problems in your head, from simple to complex: 3 + 21, 4 + 27, 6 + 123, 16 + 42, 21 + 235. Write the problems on a poster and place it at the point of sensory focus, but do not use paper to solve the problems. Find the solutions in your head. Later check your answers by doing the same problems on paper.

2) Practice the same exercise with subtraction, multiplication, and division while doing Infinity Walk.

# INTRAPERSONAL SKILLS

Self-Awareness and Insight  
Philosophical Understanding  
Integrated Body/Mind/Emotions

Both Hemispheres  
Beta, Alpha, and Theta

Intrapersonal skills take all the cognitive abilities of logical/mathematical intelligence a step further by applying them to the subject of humans' internal reality. It tackles the most profound of humankind's questions: Why do we exist? Is there a purpose to our lives? Is their existence after death? What is humankind's greatest potential? Is it obtainable in a lifetime? If there is destiny, how much control do we have over it? Who or what is God? Do thoughts create our reality? Intrapersonal intelligence explores and attempts to problem-solve the internal mysteries of life and death. Self-reflection and analysis replaces the logical/mathematical research of external objects or abstract theories about the three-dimensional world. Internal perceptions and feelings may take on greater importance than external consensus reality.

Intrapersonal abilities include creating one's own self-fulfilling prophesy through disciplined focused efforts toward specific goals; shifting moods, mental attention, and states of consciousness at will; sensing a spiritual core greater than the physical self and finding comfort in this self-awareness; and experiencing the connectedness of "Oneness" with all life.

People who are naturally talented in intrapersonal skills include philosophers, some types of mental health professionals, spiritual counselors, and many, many people living simple quiet lives of spiritual or philosophical depth. If this skill isn't naturally developed earlier in life, people are often drawn to it as they enter mid-life crisis, when the search for meaning can intensify. Late in life the urge to develop intrapersonal abilities may rise again, as the reality of death is felt more keenly. Drug and alcohol abuse is rooted in the search for shortcuts to the peace that intrapersonal mastery brings us. As with most shortcuts, the results greatly fall short of the internal awareness and experience that can be created through true intrapersonal abilities.

## Step 1. *Shifting Moods and Energy Levels*

Emotional ups and downs are a natural part of being human. We all have our quiet days and our high energy days, days we'd prefer to be alone, and days we seek out social interactions and excitement. However, when these ups or downs interfere with our life goals or our personal relationships, our emotional cycling has crossed the line from being a natural human neuro-chemical phenomenon to being a destructive force in our lives.

When we experience "downs," we are feeling a lack of energy. Each of us will label this lack of energy differently, depending on what is happening in our lives. We may call it depression, boredom, inertia, unhappiness, or feeling tired and run down.

Few of us would complain about feeling "up," because it is natural to enjoy an increase in energy. However, when we have more energy than we are able to use productively or creatively, we begin to feel nervous and even anxious. An optimal level of energy can provide us with a calm alertness, a balanced excitement, and a peaceful happiness. Infinity Walk's capacity to open and balance the nervous system can be a gift to someone experiencing too little or too much energy. If you know people whose lives are disadvantaged by emotional or physical ups and downs, share this chapter with them. (This method does not replace counseling.)

### *Too Little Energy =*

*depression, boredom, inertia, unhappiness, lack of motivation, feelings of helplessness or emptiness, chronic fatigue with no medical cause, inability to plan for the future or enjoy the present, lack of creativity, passion or fun in life, no life purpose*

If you are physically healthy, eat nutritiously, and get sufficient sleep and exercise, you should have access to large amounts of neurological energy to channel into your life goals and relationships.

If this is not the case, your energy may be tied up somewhere else within your nervous system. Just as a lack of cooperative neural networking at optimal brain wave frequencies can cause learning disabilities, it can also prevent you from accessing physical and emotional energy.

## UPLIFTING PRACTICE IDEAS FOR STEP 1.

### Television Inertia

If your inertia places you in front of a television for hours at a time, make a rule that all television viewing must be accompanied by the Infinity Walk. Don't let yourself sit down in front of the screen. If your legs tire of walking, you may lie down on the floor and do slow stretching exercises until you are ready to return to Infinity Walk. During commercials find a one minute chore to do around the house. You'll be surprised how much can be done during one minute. Some examples are to take out the garbage, to wash a few dishes, or to put the laundry in the washing machine. Plan your next one minute chore during the following television show segment.

Absolutely do not allow yourself to sit down and do nothing in front of the television. If you grow too tired to continue walking the eight pattern or do stretching exercises on the floor you must force yourself to turn off the television. Chances are, before you grow exhausted of doing the Infinity Walk in front of the television, you will have built up some incentive to work on a project around the house or to be productive in some other way.

### Daytime Napping Inertia

Short cat naps can be wonderfully refreshing. However, some people fall into a habit of taking one or more long naps a day, or going to bed unnecessarily early, as a way of avoiding unhappiness and boredom. The body can get so used to this routine that the person feels tired all the time. This perpetuates the desire for more and more sleep. In actuality, the opposite is needed. Here's what to do if you think you have fallen into a routine of sleeping too much. (Be sure a doctor has found no medical cause, first.) Before allowing yourself to take a nap you really don't need, command yourself to do Infinity Walk for a minimum of a half hour. Yes, I really do mean for a full thirty minutes. Do the walking pattern briskly to some upbeat enlivening music, or a cheerful, positive radio program. I'm suggesting this instead of watching television, because I'd like you to be using your eyes to look out at a distance. Focus out through a window, or even better, go outdoors. The further you can focus out toward the horizon line, the more you will bring your energy up and out of you, and back interacting in your environment.

When it comes to low energy slumps, you must insist on strict, unbending beta rules with yourself. Therefore, in this case, until you are over your energy slump, you never allow yourself to nap until you have first done thirty minutes of Infinity Walk, with

175

music or an upbeat radio show, while looking out at the horizon. Singing or talking out loud to yourself while doing Infinity Walk can also help release an energy slump. Don't allow yourself to nap unless you still feel physically tired after this brisk paced walking. If your physical exhaustion does not lift after following this pre-napping program for a week, be sure to talk with your family physician. Your tiredness may have an organic cause. If your doctor finds no reason for your tiredness, then read the next section on depression. You may be in a greater energy slump than you realize.

### Depression — Emotional Inertia

If you believe you are seriously depressed, reach out for help through counseling professionals or your family doctor, who can recommend proper treatment for your depression or can refer you to someone in the mental health field. Also let your family and friends know you are in need of their caring and support. In addition, I highly recommend you use what willpower you can to force yourself to do Infinity Walk to uplifting music and far distance viewing, just as outlined above. The difference is walking it for even longer periods of time to break through to the underlying cause of your depression, and to elicit positive problem-solving thoughts and behaviors. (If an unconscious cause might be difficult to deal with, be sure to get the help of a counselor.)

I have had depressed clients report that after one to two hours of a brisk paced non-stop Infinity Walk, they could actually feel a shift take place in their brains and nervous system. This shift is from a sense of feeling stuck in nothingness or negativity to having spontaneous energized insights leading to a desire to stop the eight pattern so they can go take immediate action on whatever has been bothering them. It's not uncommon for someone to just walk right out of the perpetually unending Infinity Walk pattern to do whatever they need to do to solve their present concern. Some clients have reported to me that after a time, a rush of energy to act on their problem sweeps over them and they find themselves leaving the eight pattern and heading off to some productive task before they even realize what is happening. When done intensively for one or more hours at a time, Infinity Walk becomes a moving meditation, capable to inducing profound change through a complete shift in brain wave frequencies and amplitudes.

### Too Much Non-Productive Energy =

*nervousness, anxiety, unnecessary fears and worries, obsessive thinking, tension headaches, nervous stomachs, neck and shoulder tension, inability to relax and enjoy the present moment, difficulty sleeping, lack of ease in new or social situations, inability to stop thinking, or feelings of being emotionally out of control*

Sometimes we may find ourselves overly focused on some issue in our lives, unable to bring ourselves back to a sense of peace. At these times, Infinity Walk can provide a disciplined structure through which to channel this excessive non-productive energy while giving our minds and nervous system the best possible chance of accessing our greatest mental and emotional potential, in order to work through whatever is occupying us. Infinity Walk can dissipate an emotional overcharge while balancing out the high volume of nervous energy, and can help us problem solve by giving us greater access to our full brain potential.

### ANXIETY-REDUCING PRACTICE IDEAS FOR STEP 1.

If someone is experiencing a high degree of fear or anxiety, I would suggest focusing down on the floor rather than out at a distance, while doing Infinity Walk. This cuts down on possible environmental stimulation, and helps the person stay more focused on their own internal process.

With high levels of anxiety, breathing often becomes irregular, perpetuating the feeling of being out of control. This discomfort can be eliminated while doing Infinity Walk with a slow open-mouthed yawn on the inhale, and a long, audible sigh on the exhale (see page 159). Continue this slow yawn-sigh breathing pattern as you walk very slowly, until you feel more relaxed. Keep every breath "authentic," as if each were a spontaneous yawn.

## Step 2. Power Statements and Power Walks

As Infinity Walk becomes more fluid, coordinated, and graceful for you, it will begin to activate in you a sense of personal confidence, mental clarity, and emotional balance. At this point, you may enjoy supercharging your brain through creating power statements or affirmations to use with Infinity Walk. You can review *"A Very Dynamic Morning"* on pages 52-56 for an example of how I do my own power affirmation with Infinity Walk.

Remember, to find the right affirmation for you, pay attention to how your body responds to the words as you do Infinity Walk. Feelings of being electrically charged, emotionally high, energized, joyous, hopeful, confident, etc., are signs that you have created the right statement for yourself. If your statement loses its power over time, retire it, and create a new one. As you repeat your power statement out loud, over and over, while doing Infinity Walk, be aware of walking and talking with a sense of personal power. If you are power walking, you will be walking briskly at an athletic gait, breathing easily, head held high, eyes forward rather than looking down, with a feeling of strength, solidity, and centeredness down through your arms and legs. Your voice will reflect the power in your movements, supporting and enhancing your chosen power statement.

Forget about appearing dainty. Let your walk feel solidly anchored to the ground. Feel the solidity of the earth or the floor come up through your legs. Feel firmly rooted to the earth, so that nothing could knock you off balance. (Use your toes to grip the floor as you walk.) Every arm swing in the power walk should feel deliberate. Feel yourself willing your body's movement forward as you do Infinity Walk. Imagine in your lower body the strength and solidity of an oak tree deeply rooted into the earth, and, in your upper body the grace and flexibility of the top branches reaching toward the sun.

If you can stay aware of your power walk, while you audibly affirm yourself through your power statements, your Infinity Walk will become a source of great personal transformation for you. Affirmations can focus on physical or mental excellence, emotional freedom and balance, or spiritual awareness in your daily living. Done daily, you will have created a very simple method to give yourself optimal preparation for getting the most out of each day.

### SUMMARY
### NO LIMITS

There's no limit to the sensory and motor complexities that you can add to Infinity Walk, or the number of these neurological complexities you can do simultaneously while walking the eight pattern. Don't stop here; continue to create additional neurological challenges for your special needs and interests.

Infinity Walk can provide you with the neurological foundation for any challenge you wish to meet during your life. You can never outgrow it; by continuing to add further sensory and motor complexities, it will grow with you. I hope you will invest enough time into developing your Infinity Walk to begin to realize some of its neurological benefits to you. The more you put into it, the more it will be able to provide you with increased neurological sophistication and help you reach your personal goals and fulfill your dreams.

CHAPTER 12

# Closing Thoughts

## WORKING WITH STUDENTS WHO ALREADY FEEL DEFEATED

After you have a good, basic understanding of the concepts in Infinity Walk, you will be ready to start using the principles for your own enrichment as well as for that of your students. Here are some of my thoughts on what makes the difference between success and failure in using these methods with students who have given up.

It's important that you experience all levels of the work in Part I, II, and III of *Infinity Walk* before teaching them to someone else. Reading methodology is not enough; you'll need to experience the value of Infinity Walk through your own body before you'll be able to help someone else through the program. Also, you will be shortchanging yourself if you skip putting yourself through the Infinity Walk program. (Workshops taught by myself are available if you would like more instruction than a book can offer.)

When it comes to a brain, no one has more understanding than the owner of the head. Therefore, the old way of just teaching content cannot work here. If you choose to do this work, you will only succeed if you can willingly take your place next to each student as their equal. Why do I say this? If you do not give the authority and responsibility to learn back to the students, they will not open up and teach you how their minds work. Instead, they will continue taking a passive role, expecting you to know.

Sharing your enthusiasm over what you have discovered about your own brain will encourage students to explore their own potential inner treasures. At first, this self-discovery process will need to be demonstrated through your own and others' experiences. However, once they grasp the ideas in *Infinity Walk,* many students will become self-motivated in their efforts.

You may get only one chance to catch a defeated student's interest. Therefore, make your first session a highly energized discovery time. Keep assessment to a minimum, and do nothing to embarrass or draw attention to an academic weak point. Focus only on the student's potentials and present strengths. Interact with each student as a precious human being with a unique mind. This is your opportunity to learn something from this special person and to share your own specialness. Let go of any illusion of having more to offer than to gain. Think larger than grade level, content learning, and academic success. These are not measurements of value as a human being.

Be patient. Some of these students have been emotionally wounded by their labeled inferiority or situations out of their control. We are not born into this world with a deficiency in motivation. An unmotivated student is always, always a deeply hurting person.

Students who hurt cannot be expected to be enthusiastic about learning, any more than you can be expected to perform well at work when you are suffering from flu symptoms. Even with all your efforts, these students will still need to heal at their own pace. Once your gentle and enthusiastic efforts have brought them to a point of self-confidence and motivation, their academic gains should begin picking up speed. Until this point, any forcing may be fruitless, and even harmful.

*Stress that the Infinity Walk program helps develop the whole brain, so it's good for everyone.* It isn't just for students with "problems." Prove this to them by telling them how it has helped you, or someone you know. Tell them that after they learn the Infinity Walk Sensorimotor Program they can teach it to their families and friends. Students will quickly get the idea that something very new and different is in the air, and increased motivation will follow. Once you succeed in reaching a defeated student's mind, genuine rapport and mutual respect can develop, paving the way for exciting self-discoveries for both of you.

## SOLVING TODAY'S CRISIS IN EDUCATION

We have reached a point in America's history where the average student's mind simply isn't primed for academic learning. I don't need to go into all the possible reasons for this; the crisis in American education has been well covered by news media these last few years. Schools are under pressure to bring up the standardized test scores of their students. Teachers who already feel overburdened are asked to give even more of themselves. American industry is concerned that tomorrow's employees won't be sufficiently educated to be an asset to their companies. Parents are at wit's end, trying to understand why their children aren't learning in school when they seem to be bright outside the classroom.

In reading *Infinity Walk,* you may have already begun to understand the cause of this crisis. Students are not absorbing two-dimensional information as well as past generations have. Rather than looking for someone or something to blame for this change, let's look at what this really means. (1) Children are naturally three-dimensional in their perceptions and understandings of life. (2) In the past, many children turned away from developing their three-dimensional capacities in order to focus on mastering the two-dimensional realm. (3) Children's minds are not catching on to the reality of two dimensions as well as they used to.

Does this have to be a crisis? Instead of blaming the problem on drugs, sugar products, television, single parenting, and burned out teachers, let's fantasize for a minute. Let's imagine that our children's generation is part of a transition phase in the evolution of humankind. Let's imagine that in future generations, the battle between two-dimensional knowledge and three-dimensional intuition will end, with the merging of the two realms into one consciousness. Let's imagine that this evolutionary transition requires the human brain to recognize two dimensions as an aspect of the three-dimensional world, rather than as a totally separate — and sometimes conflicting — reality.

If we can imagine this, then there is no crisis in education, because the solution becomes painlessly easy. Teach to the students' three-dimensional minds, and the learning will come naturally. Even two-dimensional language and symbols can be absorbed by presenting them from a three-dimensional perspective. Many creative educators, past and present, have known this "secret."

While we're fantasizing, I'd like to play Empress of Education for a few minutes. Here's my list of how I would accomplish three-dimensional education. It's based on my three-dimensional experience with students who could not learn two-dimensionally, and on my own childhood observations throughout my school years. Perhaps you can add to this list.

## 1.  TEACHING HOW TO LEARN

I would add a curriculum on How to Learn. Many students need to be taught how to visualize in three dimensions; and some even need guidance in how to feel deeply about life and all it has to offer. Only then can their rich three-

181

dimensional senses (alpha) and feelings of empathy (theta) be applied to the required content curriculum. Without adding these necessary inner dimensions of experience to academic content, alpha and theta will not be activated. Many excellent ideas for a "How to Learn" curriculum can be found in books such as *The Learning Revolution* by Gordon Dryden and Jeannette Vos; and *Superlearning 2000* by Sheila Ostrander and Lynn Schroeder.

## 2.  SELF-EXPLORATION OF ONE'S OWN NEUROLOGICAL UNIQUENESS

I would include in the How to Learn curriculum an experiential lab to allow the students to learn about their own present sensorimotor pattern as well as how to expand their present sensorimotor pattern through the Oneness + 2-D + 3-D formula to realize their full potential.

I've never seen discouraged students perk up faster than when I've introduced the concept of how their unique brains work. All of a sudden they feel on top of things again. When I show them how to use their particular brain dominance patterns to learn, a new desire to succeed is born. When I point out reasons — in a way that makes sense to them — that their brains haven't handled certain types of information in the past, they feel in control again.

References: Dryden & Vos, *The Learning Revolution*, Jalmar Press, CA: 1994; Sheila Ostrander and Lynn Schroeder, *Superlearning 2000*, Delacorte Press, NY: 1994.

The sting of failure comes from not knowing how to change failure to success. Self-esteem does an instant turn-around and students eagerly take back the responsibility to develop their own brains as soon as these pupils are shown the way to reach their neurological potential. What seems to excite them most is a new sense of control in their lives; they set out to learn something, and they do!

## 3.  THE EDUCATION INDUSTRY CAN HELP

To aid the busy teacher, all textbooks and commercial teaching materials would address the students' need to creatively approach the content from curiosity. In addition, how the content applies to important aspects of the "real" three-dimensional world would be spelled out. If the content is not important to life, why should the student be motivated to absorb it? If they are aware of the need, the educational publishing industry will be very willing to accept the creative challenge of bringing alpha-related perceptions and theta-related values and motivation into the beta content of the teaching materials. Teachers who order books and materials from publishing companies that choose to take the challenge will reinforce the production of more materials of this quality.

## 4.  TEACHING THE TEACHERS

All teacher colleges would have curriculum on (a) teaching to the three-dimensional mind rather than just focusing on two-dimensional content; (b) developing visual and other forms of sensory imagination as part of class instruction; (c) using the classroom to help students discover their own specialness; (d) integrating the principles of Oneness + 2-D + 3-D into all content teachings; and (e) using the Infinity Walk Sensorimotor Program to help students develop the neurological means to demonstrate their knowledge.

## 5.  TAKING THE DULL OUT OF TWO-DIMENSIONAL

Some subjects that appear to be only two-dimensional, such as spelling, the multiplication table, and high school algebra, need an important three-dimensional motivation applied to them. *When students ask why they need to learn something, it's because their minds need a strong three-dimensional motivator in order to absorb the material more easily.* Sometimes that motivator can be learning how to learn, developing a superior brain, exercising their brain the way they exercise their muscles, developing a powerful mind that can survive against all odds, or reaching their career dream. Everyone has their own reasons for wanting to develop their maximum brain potential. Find those reasons and you have tapped into the motivation behind absorbing two-dimensional symbols.

Today's students, for whatever reason, are not like past generations. It is no longer enough to teach content, because many of them don't have the slightest idea how to learn it. Today's students must be helped to understand that their brains are a creative energy system with unknown potential so vast that we may never discover a limit to our potential.

I've seen the best of traditional educational programs fail to make the difference with highly motivated "learning disabled" students who had exceptional teacher and parental support. Their progress, in spite of so much effort, was frustratingly slow. Each success was such a struggle that it was hard for these students to muster up enthusiasm in light of all the drilling yet to come.

It's all so unnecessary. When the neuro-pathways are open and made ready, learning becomes so much easier that it sometimes appears magical. How can something be so difficult one day, and so easy the next? Simple, by opening the door before trying to walk through it. The single most important function that formal education can perform is giving students the key that opens that door.

# Index

---
## INFORMATION FORM
---

return to

**Jalmar Press**
**24426 S. Main Street, Suite 702**
**Carson, CA 90745**

## *Training and Income Opportunities*

Dr. Sunbeck tours the country teaching *Infinity Walk*, and is available for lectures, workshops, professional training intensives, private sessions, and continuing education college courses. Write for more information.

_____ I'd like information on Dr. Sunbeck's planned tours.

_____ I'd like information on being a paid sponsor for Dr. Sunbeck's visit to my community.

_____ I'd like information on selling *Infinity Walk* books and videos for profit in my community.

_____ I'd like information on continuing education credit.

_____ I'd like information on training in Infinity Walk.

_____ I'd like information on private sessions in Rochester, New York.

_____ I'd like information on training in and purchasing the *EEG biofeedback equipment* mentioned in Chapter 5.

Please <u>Print</u> or <u>Type</u> Only

Name _____ Address _____

City _____ State _____ Zip _____

Phone ( ) _____

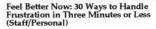